Hardy's Love Poems

Carl J. Weber was Professor Emeritus of English Literature at Colby College, Maine, USA, and a noted Hardy scholar. His books include *Hardy of Wessex: a Centennial Biography*, *The First Hundred Years of Thomas Hardy: a Bibliography*, *Hardy Music*, *Hardy in America*, *Hardy and the Lady from Madison Square* and *The Rise and Fall of James Ripley Osgood*. In addition, he edited four of Hardy's novels, *Hardy's 'Lost' Novel*, *Hardy's Uncollected Tales*, *Hardy's Letters* and *Dearest Emmie: Thomas Hardy's Letters to His First Wife*.

Hardy's
Love Poems

edited with notes and an introduction by
Carl J. Weber

MACMILLAN LONDON

First published 1963 by Macmillan and Company Limited

First published in paperback 1983 by
PAPERMAC
a division of Macmillan Publishers Limited
4 Little Essex Street London WC2R 3LF
and Basingstoke

Associated companies in Auckland, Dallas,
Delhi, Dublin, Hong Kong, Johannesburg,
Lagos, Manzini, Melbourne, Nairobi,
New York, Singapore, Tokyo, Washington
and Zaria

ISBN 0 333 34798 6

Printed by Redwood Burn Limited, Trowbridge

PREFACE

IF students of English literature were challenged to name the best three series of love poems in English, there would probably be very little hesitation, in any company of qualified judges, in naming at least *two* : Elizabeth Barrett Browning's *Sonnets from the Portuguese* and Shakespeare's *Sonnets*. There might be some argument among the judges as to whether to put Mrs. Browning first and Shakespeare second, or whether to put Shakespeare first and Mrs. Browning second, but there is little room for doubt that the sonnet-sequences of both poets would appear in any list of the best love poems in English.

But what series would be named in third place ? Wordsworth's poems to Lucy, like Matthew Arnold's similarly challenging poems to Marguerite, are (in spite of their interest and their fame) too few, too slight, too lacking in coherent unity, to qualify for admittance to so select a company as the best three. Rossetti's *House of Life* might appeal to some, but this series of sonnets is just as certain *not* to appeal to others. The claims of George Meredith's *Modern Love* might be zealously urged by some admirers, but the tart tang of this sequence of poems would doubtless lead many to vote against it. And to what series of love poems are we to turn next in our search for a candidate for the number three position ?

The present editor's nomination of Thomas Hardy's 'Poems of 1912–13' may surprise some readers, but what may seem to them of even more questionable soundness is the editor's judgment that, in some respects, Hardy's

v

poems deserve to be ranked, not third, but first. 'In *some* respects', I say, and this qualification calls of course for some explanation.

No lover of poetry will claim that, in the expression of fervid devotion, Hardy is to be ranked ahead of Elizabeth Barrett Browning. Her position *there* is assured. And no qualified judge will be so foolish as to claim that, in the creation of that 'fine frenzy' which distinguishes the work of Shakespeare's pen from that of all rivals, the man from Dorset could equal, let alone excel, the man from Warwickshire. But Thomas Hardy accomplished a number of things that neither Mrs. Browning nor Shakespeare attempted. His verses therefore represent, as love poems, an achievement not attained by either of the other two. Elizabeth Barrett's ardour was poured forth into the fervent lines of her sonnets during the year 1845–46 which preceded her marriage to Robert Browning, and with that marriage the poems ceased. There is therefore a unity, a concentrated and harmonious singleness of purpose, and an intensity of effect that distinguish the *Sonnets from the Portuguese* from all other love poems in English. Shakespeare's, by contrast, are dispersed and discursive. They lack unity. Their composition is spread over a longer period in the poet's life and the sonnets are not addressed to a single individual. Some of them are little more than rhetorical exercises, full of puns and verbal tricks.

Thomas Hardy's 'Poems of 1912–13' — and the nearly one hundred other poems which belong with them and should be read with them — Hardy's 'Poems' are *not* rhetorical exercises. They record actual experiences of the poet, but experiences of far greater extent and variety than those recorded by Shakespeare or Mrs. Browning. Hardy, like Mrs. Browning, begins with the magic glow of courtship ; but whereas her forty-four poems are the result of forty-two weeks (more or less), *his* are the record of forty-two *years*. Whereas Shakespeare's *Sonnets* testify to his ardent devotion and to his reckless infatuation, they stop short long before the end of the poet's life, or even of his *affaire*. Hardy's poems, on the other hand, run the gamut—from first sight of the loved one, through courtship, to marriage, to quarrel, to staled familiarity, to disillusion, to bitterness and 'division', and finally to death, and thereafter to self-examination, remorse, expiation, and the rebirth of love. In short, Hardy's poems provide a complete summary of his adult life in a way that neither Shakespeare's nor Mrs. Browning's attempt. Mrs. Browning did not live long enough to write any sonnets on Robert's proposal of marriage to Louisa Lady Ashburton, and Shakespeare wrote no poetical lines on his notorious testamentary second-best bed.

This autobiographical inclusiveness on Hardy's part is, of course, not necessarily a *poetical* virtue. One does not measure the quality of poetry by the number of years over which the poems are spread. But what justifies us in making high claims for Hardy's love poems is the intensity, the originality, the tenderness, the poignancy, the delicacy, the wistfulness — in short, the emotional range — that they exhibit. They are not all alike ; they are not homogeneous ; they are not merely the record of a honeymoon in a poet's life. They are life itself ; they cover all of life and cover it with clarity and poetic charm.

Each reader of the following pages will be able to judge for himself whether these claims for the high merits of Hardy's poems are justified or not, and no time need be spent here and now in arguing about them. The poems will speak for themselves. What *is* here needed, I believe, is an explanation of why Hardy's 'Poems of 1912–13' have hitherto not been better known by the general reader. There are three reasons :

First of all, the title of the series carries no special appeal to a reader — particularly to one unaware of the calendrical facts that the first Mrs. Hardy died in 1912 and that these poems were written in the months immediately following her death. Second, when these verses were first published, they were tucked into the middle of a book called *Satires of Circumstance, Lyrics, and Reveries* in which the satires, with their astringent quality, attracted much more attention than the reveries. Moreover, that volume was, unfortunately, published in 1914 shortly after the outbreak of a world war during which English readers had other things to do besides read love poetry.

Now that fifty more years have passed, we have a better chance not only to set Hardy's 'ancient flame' in its proper setting, but also to supplement the 'Poems of 1912–13' with the others which he published elsewhere — either in other parts of the same 1914 volume, or in one or another of the four subsequently published volumes of his poetry. In all, there are nearly six-score poems inspired by Thomas Hardy's love for Emma Lavinia Gifford.

These records of his Cornish romance call for one further preliminary comment. Their emotional range and variety are reflected in a paralleling profusion of metres and stanzaic forms. The metres harmonize with the emotions. Whereas Shakespeare's and Mrs. Browning's poems are, in one respect, all alike — *i.e.* they are all in sonnet-form — Hardy's are not only *not* all alike, but offer such variety, such charm, such delicacy, and show such metrical dexterity, such resourcefulness in fitting the techniques of verse to the varied moods of the poet, as to surprise any reader who will take the trouble to examine carefully the art displayed in their composition. There are long lines and short lines, there are iambic rhythms and dactylic and anapestic rhythms as well; there are ballad stanzas and simple lyrics; there are narratives and 'laments'; monosyllabic lines are contrasted with polysyllabic; dramatic shifts in tempo are managed with the consummate skill born of Hardy's youthful experience in playing the violin. Alliteration and assonance, single rhymes, double and even triple rhymes, are all handled, not only with ability, but with such individuality of touch as to belie almost every suggestion of indebtedness to other poets. Any student of Hardy's *Collected Poems* will have no great difficulty in discovering that Hardy went to school to Shelley and Browning, to Swinburne and Shakespeare, and that he knew Wordsworth and Keats, Poe and Walt Whitman. In many of his poems, Hardy's technical indebtedness to his teachers is easily discernible. But in these love poems — all of them the direct product of his own experience — he writes from the heart, and writes with a sincerity and sureness of touch that fully justify the high claims here made for these poems. 'For out of the abundance of the heart the mouth speaketh.'

Although anyone who owns the *Collected Poems* can find all the verses inspired by Miss Gifford scattered through its pages, these poems have never before been assembled as here, *i.e.* segregated and presented as a biographical unit. This book is, in short, the first attempt to set the poems clearly and directly against the background of fact, and so let the poet's experience of love elucidate his verse, and his poems thus illuminate his life.

Bibliographical information about individual poems

is given in the notes that follow the introduction, and details about Hardy's various volumes of verse will be found at the beginning of these notes. On a number of pages in the introduction, the editor has availed himself of some of his own previously-published statements or comments ; that is to say, he has lifted some sentences from his centennial biography of Hardy and has also here paraphrased or has, at times, reprinted verbatim certain passages in 'Dearest Emmie' (1963). This paraphrasing or repeating has been done in order to make the present volume an independent work, on the assumption that there may be readers who would prefer not to delay an examination of the poetry here printed while hunting up a copy of the volume of letters which has been issued as a preliminary volume. Any reader who has already acquainted himself with the editorial comments in 'Dearest Emmie' will know what can be safely skipped in the pages that follow in the present volume. Other books to which reference is made or from which brief quotations have been taken are identified in the bibliography which precedes the indexes.

The editor makes grateful acknowledgment of the help given him by Mr. T. M. Farmiloe in the London office of Macmillan and Company, and by Miss Irene Cooper Willis, Trustee (with Lloyds Bank) of the Hardy Estate. While these collaborators are in no way responsible for whatever flaws or defects may remain in this book, it is a better production than it would have been without their wise and efficient aid.

C. J. W.

CONTENTS

xi

HARDY'S CORNISH ROMANCE

I

JOURNEY INTO LYONNESSE

EARLY on Monday morning, 7 March 1870, lights appeared
long before daylight in the thatched cottage on the western
edge of Puddletown Heath — that 'vast tract of unen-
closed wild' which was destined to become known as
Egdon Heath as soon as *The Return of the Native* had made
its way in the world. Thomas Hardy never forgot that
morning or that day. 'What rainbow rays embow it !'
he exclaimed many years later.

'On the morning of departure he rose at half-past
three, for . . . it was necessary to start early. . . . The
candle-flame had a sad and yellow look when it was
brought into his bedroom. . . . Few things will take
away a man's confidence in an impulsive scheme more
than being called up by candlelight upon a chilly morning to commence working it out. But . . . he overcame
his weakness and bustled out of bed.'[1]*

Hardy soon finished the breakfast his mother had prepared for him, and by four o'clock he was ready to depart
on his journey. He put on his overcoat — a rather shabby
one — bade his mother good-bye, and 'stepped from the
door' of the thatched cottage. 'The morning was dark,
and the raw wind made him shiver till walking warmed
him. "Good heavens, here's an undertaking !" he
thought. Old trees seemed to look at him through the
gloom, as they rocked uneasily to and fro. . . . The dead

* Notes and references are printed collectively at the end of this
Introduction. See page 89.

I

leaves in the ditches, which could be heard but not seen, shifted their position with a troubled rustle.' [1]

This alertness to the sound of the dead leaves and this familiarity with trees that 'seemed to look at him' was an old experience for Hardy, for he had been walking that road for twenty years — ever since he was nine. He knew every inch of it, and knew it by sound as well as by sight. Only two years before he set out on his journey on this raw March morning in 1870, he had written :

> To dwellers in a wood, almost every species of tree has its voice as well as its feature. At the passing of the breeze the fir-trees sob and moan no less distinctly than they rock ; the holly whistles as it battles with itself ; the ash hisses amid its quiverings ; the beech rustles while its flat boughs rise and fall. And winter, which modifies the note of such trees as shed their leaves, does not destroy its individuality. . . . The lonely lane he was following connected one of the hamlets of Mellstock parish with Upper Mellstock . . . and to his eyes, casually glancing upward, the silver and black-stemmed birches with their characteristic tufts, the pale gray boughs of beech, the dark-creviced elm, all appeared now as black and flat outlines upon the sky, wherein the white stars twinkled. [2]

The unique knowledge of trees here shown eventually became known to all who made Hardy's acquaintance, and the day eventually arrived when Sir James Barrie could declare : 'Everyone knows that he had an intimacy with trees . . . and . . . the trees had a similar knowledge of him. . . . When he passed through their wood, they could tell him from all other men !' [3]

If we look more closely at the words quoted above from Hardy's writings, we notice that there is an undercurrent of melancholy in them, an absence of enthusiasm in him. The candle-flame had a sad look ; the raw wind made him shiver ; the trees rocked uneasily through the gloom ; the dead leaves moved with a troubled rustle ; the fir trees sobbed and moaned. Even an inexperienced and unskilful psychologist could have deduced that Thomas Hardy, then twenty-nine years old, carried with him a troubled heart, or at least a diffident mind. 'Few things will take away a man's confidence more than being called up by candlelight upon a chilly morning.'

As he strode along toward Dorchester, Hardy had abundant opportunity for thinking back over the past ten years of his life and for finding little reason for joy in the retrospect. Things had not gone well with him. Two years before this March walk he had memorized Shakespeare's third sonnet, and had learned to apply to himself the poet's plaintive accusation of Fortune : 'The guilty goddess . . . that did not better for my life provide.' Hardy felt that, in the course of the past eight years, he had been buffeted and beaten and bruised—so much so, that, as early as 1866, while he was living in London, he had written a Shakespearean sonnet of his own in which he lamented that 'Time, for gladness, casts a moan'. Joy lay slain, he declared ; and the worst of it was that the moaning and the pain were without reason or proper cause. Fortune might, so he thought, have just 'as readily strown/Blisses about my pilgrimage as pain'.[4] No wonder he found little cause for enthusiasm as he proceeded on his way that cold March morning ! The habit of feeling sorry for himself had already become fixed.

By 4.30 Hardy was passing within a few hundred yards of Stinsford Church, but the night was too dark for him to be able to make out, off to his left, the Gothic tower of the venerable church which he had attended as a boy. We are to hear much more about Stinsford Church later. He shortly emerged upon the main highway into

3

Dorchester. As he approached the silent town, he had to cross two bridges : the first built of stone ; the second, of weatherstained brick. How well he knew them both ! How many hundreds of times he had crossed them on his way to or from school and had noticed the 'marked difference of quality between the personages who haunted the bridge of brick and the personages who haunted the bridge of stone'. His long experience in Dorchester had taught him that 'to this pair of bridges gravitated all the failures of the town. . . . Those of lowest character preferred the brick bridge, adjoining the town ; they did not mind the glare of the public eye. The *misérables* who would pause on the stone bridge were of a politer stamp. . . . The eyes of this species were mostly over the parapet upon the running water below.' [5]

At the early hour of 7 March when Hardy crossed Gray's Bridge — the one built of stone — there were no loiterers on hand, but the sound of the water as it flowed under the arches and between the piers of the bridge gave him reason enough for sober thought. For off to the right, almost within stone's throw of the bridge, lay Ten Hatches Weir ; and, as he liked (in after years) to tell visitors to Dorchester, 'Ten Hatches Weir was always a favourite spot for suicides'.[6] In the early-morning darkness Hardy could hear the water gurgling through the weirs.

He now mounted High Street to the grizzled old church of St. Peter's and there turned left, proceeded down South Street, and shortly passed the building where he had served his six-year apprenticeship under architect John Hicks. Near by was the school taught by the Reverend William Barnes, the Dorset poet. A few minutes' further walking brought Hardy to 'the Ring'. This was 'the local name of one of the finest Roman

Amphitheatres, if not the very finest, remaining in Britain'.[7]

A few more minutes of striding along the empty and silent highway, and then the young architect turned off from South Street and made his way to the railway station. It was not yet five o'clock. He had timed his walk perfectly, and was on hand when the first train of the morning arrived to pick him up and transport him to the next town, only a dozen or so miles away. There he had to change trains, and as the first faint light began to appear in the eastern sky, the traveller was riding along north of Beaminster on his way to Yeovil Junction.

The countryside was still too dark for him to make out many of its features, and his thoughts could therefore the more easily turn in upon themselves. His recent purchase of several volumes of Bohn's Classical Series had included *Marcus Aurelius*. In the pages of this Roman philosopher Hardy had marked : 'This is the chief thing : Be not perturbed'. It is easy to *say* that ; but he *was* perturbed, and he could not help it.

The curious fact is that, on this cold March morning, Hardy was more interested in reading poetry and in trying to compose verses of his own than he was in the business of his errand. As the train rumbled on toward Yeovil, he had time to recall his futile attempts to get his poems published, and to remember the bitter day when he wrote in his notebook : 'The world does not despise us ; it only neglects us'.

Upon arriving at Yeovil Junction, the brooding young man had to change trains once again ; and as he sat there in the station, glumly waiting for the arrival of the London-to-Exeter train, he had (we may well believe) 'the hard, half-apathetic expression of one who deems anything possible at the hands of Time and Chance except, perhaps, fair play'.[8] Later publications by him enable us to picture him as trying to take his mind off gloomy thoughts by reverting to the verse-making habits of his London days. Just as Wordsworth had once composed a famous poem while on a walking tour to Tintern Abbey, so Hardy could now try to describe *his* morning's walk in metre. He was now on his way to Cornwall, the poetic name of which was Lyonnesse. We can picture Hardy meditating on the various things he had noticed on his early walk, and can see him eventually pull a piece of paper from his pocket, and on it write :

> When I set out for Lyonnesse
>   A hundred miles away,
>   The rime was on the spray,
> And starlight lit my lonesomeness
> When I set out for Lyonnesse
>   A hundred miles away.

When the train from London coasted into the station, the traveller thrust the paper into his overcoat pocket.

By this time, the sky had become light enough so that, as Hardy proceeded on his way westward, the countryside offered varied rewards to his observant eyes. The well-groomed hills of Devonshire were more striking than the Dorset landscape familiar to the eyes of the would-be poet, and as the train rolled on toward Exeter there was plenty to attract his attention.

At Exeter there was another change of trains, with a further need to wait in the station ; and then, as the afternoon wore on, there was a slower ride skirting the heights of Dartmoor. Eventually the train entered Cornwall, and the landscape became coarser and rougher. At Launceston Hardy alighted, inquired where he might hire a conveyance to take him some fifteen or sixteen miles farther, and eventually found a man who had often driven over to

St. Juliot, and who now agreed to transport Hardy thither by a horse-drawn four-wheeler. This proved to be a tedious, slow trip of several hours. The roads were primitive, the lanes narrow, the hills steep. The light had already faded from the March sky before the driver, after skirting Boscastle, turned down a lane narrower than any yet, and finally announced that they were at last approaching St. Juliot.

'So it's the rectory ye are going to ?' he asked.

'Yes,' replied the young architect. 'Do you know the present incumbent ?'

'The Reverend Caddell Holder ? No ; but I've often driven to the rectory before he came.'

'How long has he been here ?'

'Oh, maybe about a year, or a year and half : 'tisn't two years ; for they don't scandalize him yet ; and, as a rule, a parish begins to scandalize the parson at the end of two years.' 9

The sky had by now become quite black, but the horse had little opportunity to stray from the route ; for the lane was so narrow and the mounds of earth on either side of the lane were so high that progress, if slow, was at least safe. At last, at a turning in the lane, the outline of a dilapidated Gothic church could be dimly discerned to the right, and near by stood, presumably, the rectory.

The architect paid off the man from Launceston, then stepped to the door of the dwelling and rang the bell. The door was shortly opened by a maid.

'I am Thomas Hardy,' he said ; and when these words seemed to convey no meaning to the maid, he added : '— the architect from Dorchester, sent by Mr. Crickmay. This is Mr. Holder's rectory, is it not ?'

'Yes,' replied the maid ; 'won't you come in ?'

Thomas Hardy entered the house where Fortune,

whom he had accused of being a guilty goddess, had all this time been preparing a great surprise for him.

> What would bechance at Lyonnesse
> While I should sojourn there
> No prophet durst declare,
> Nor did the wisest wizard guess
> What would bechance at Lyonnesse
> While I should sojourn there.[10]

As soon as the maid admitted Hardy to the rectory at St. Juliot, he was welcomed by the rector's sister-in-law, Miss Emma Lavinia Gifford. In writing his memoranda regarding the events of that day, Hardy needed only six words to describe his arrival : 'Received by young lady in brown'. She was then twenty-nine years old, half a year younger than he. She informed him that the rector was ill, and that his wife was, at the moment, attending him upstairs. Hence the architect had to be received by Mrs. Holder's sister.

Miss Gifford noticed Hardy's soft voice, his 'slightly different accent', his beard, which made him look much older than he really was, and his 'rather shabby greatcoat', and she noticed, too, that there was 'a blue paper sticking out of his pocket'. She thought it might be a design for the church-tower, which was the occasion for the architect's visit, but Hardy informed her that it was the manuscript of a poem. This surprised her. So this architect wrote poems !

Exactly what poem he did not tell her. Nor does anyone really *know*. In the preceding chapter it has been suggested that, on this 7th day of March 1870, Hardy began composing 'When I Set Out For Lyonnesse', but there is no proof that this was the poem which Miss Gifford saw 'sticking out of his pocket'. Readers who are aware of the fact that 'When I Set Out' was not published until 1914 may well be sceptical about the identity of the 1870 composition. But this scepticism can be moderated by noting the evidence that, as he travelled that day, Hardy was dreaming of a woman and not of a church tower. Let the reader recall Hardy's note, written down five years previously, on the evening of his twenty-fifth birthday : 'Wondered what woman, if any, I should be thinking about in five years' time' (Early Life, p. 65), and then supplement that note by reading 'The Wind's Prophecy' in which Hardy tells us that, now that the five years were about up, he was day-dreaming about a 'lady's . . . ebon loops of hair' while he was journeying on toward the Cornish rectory where, all unknown to him, there awaited him another lady with 'tresses flashing fair'.[1]

Miss Gifford later recorded the fact that, on that seventh day of March, she 'must confess' to having had 'a curiosity . . . as to what the architect would be like'. Her feelings about the expected arrival were later versified by Hardy himself in 'A Man Was Drawing Near to Me' :

> There was a rumble at the door,
> A draught disturbed the drapery,
> And but a minute passed before,
> > With gaze that bore
> > My destiny,
> The man revealed himself to me.[2]

In 'The Discovery' Hardy subsequently described how he had 'wandered to a crude coast . . . and . . . never once guessed' that there a young lady lived — one whom 'my heart could not but follow'.[3] Every sight seen by him on that day-of-discovery was indelibly recorded in his memory — even to the 'smiling' inn at Launceston where he 'hired horse and man for bearing me on my wayfaring'.[4]

After the evening meal, the 'young lady in brown' played some music and sang. Following this pleasant Monday evening, there ensued a week of unclouded delight. The weather was dry and warm — surprisingly so for March. On Tuesday the 8th, Hardy was busy all day at the church, examining, measuring, sketching. On Wednesday the 9th, he drove with Mrs. Holder and Miss Gifford to inspect several near-by slate quarries, and in this way became acquainted with Penpethy, Tintagel, and Boscastle. Throughout all his after-life, he never saw green slates without recalling that visit of 9 March with Miss Gifford to Penpethy :

> And now, though fifty years have flown . . .
> Green slates — seen high on roofs, or lower
> In waggon, truck, or lorry —
> Cry out : 'Our home was where you saw her
> Standing in the quarry !' [5]

On the drive back from Boscastle, the road proved too steep in one place for the carriage with three passengers. Hardy and Miss Gifford 'alighted to ease the sturdy pony's load'. Leaving Mrs. Holder to drive the chaise up the hill, the other two walked. In the poem 'At Castle Boterel' Hardy tells what happened :

> It filled but a minute. But was there ever
> A time of such quality, since or before,
> In that hill's story ? To one mind, never.[6]

That hill's 'story' remained in his memory to the end of his life. In 'A Dream or No' he recognizes that 'much of my life' claims the country near St. Juliot 'as its key', and the

> maiden abiding
> Thereat as in hiding,
> Fair-eyed and white-shouldered, broad-browed and
> brown-tressed [7]

'quickly . . . drew me. . .' Hardy's notes on this week show what the word 'quickly' in the poem meant to him.

On Monday it was the 'young lady in brown'. On Wednesday : 'Drove with . . . Miss Gifford to Boscastle'. By Thursday she had become 'E. L. G.'

On Wednesday evening the two sisters sang duets. In 'A Duettist to her Pianoforte' Hardy identifies some of the songs played that March evening.[8] 'Every sound moves memories', he wrote.

The events of the next morning, Thursday, 10 March, left this record among Hardy's notes : 'Went with E. L. G. to Beeny Cliff. She on horseback. . . . On the cliff. . . . "The tender grace of a day," etc.' Her notes supplement his : 'I rode my pretty mare Fanny and he walked by my side'. Miss Gifford's father had taught her how to ride, but she now discovered that Hardy did not even know how to help her to mount. Other little points, dropped in conversation, served to call his attention to the difference in their backgrounds. Readers of 'An Indiscretion in the Life of an Heiress' will probably not be very far wrong if they suspect that, in the dialogue between Egbert and Geraldine, a reminiscence of a conversation between E. L. G. and Thomas Hardy is to be heard :

'How long does it take to go to Westcombe ?'
'About two hours.'
'Two hours — so long as that ? How far is it away ?'
'Eight miles.'
'Two hours to drive eight miles — who ever heard of such a thing !'
'I thought you meant walking.'
'Ah, yes ; but one hardly means walking without expressly stating it.'
'Well, it seems just the other way to me — that walking is meant unless you say driving.'

Thus they both became conscious of 'their differing habits and . . . contrasting positions which could not be reconciled. Indeed, this perception of their disparity weighed more and more heavily . . . as the days went on. . . .' The words — and the perception — were prophetic.

For the time being, however, Hardy enjoyed walking while E. L. G. rode her mare Fanny. That trip to Beeny Cliff resulted (forty-three years later) in one of Hardy's most lilting lyrics :

> O the opal and the sapphire of that wandering western
> sea,
> And the woman riding high above with bright hair
> flapping free —
> The woman whom I loved so, and who loyally loved
> me.[9]

This poem was long in emerging from the recesses of Hardy's memory, but only three years after this first visit to Beeny Cliff, he made use of it in one of the most famous chapters of *A Pair of Blue Eyes*.

In 'The Phantom Horsewoman' Hardy recalls E. L. G. as a 'girl-rider' and imagines that

> she still rides gaily
> In his rapt thought
> On that shaggèd and shaly
> Atlantic spot . . .
> Draws rein and sings to the swing of the tide.[10]

In 'Places' he recalls how, at Boterel Hill 'where the waggoners skid',

> She cantered down, as if she must fall
> (Though she never did). . . .[11]

Thursday evening, after the return to St. Juliot from the cliff, there was more music after dinner. Miss Gifford, wearing a 'gown of fading fashion',

> sang with lips that trembled
> 'Shall I see his face again ?' [12]

The next morning, she struck a light six times in her anxiety to call the servants early enough to get the architect off on time for his return journey. Hardy's poem 'The Frozen Greenhouse' tells us something about that morning. 'There was a frost last night', she said at the breakfast table. The room was lit by candles because of the early hour. 'The stove was forgot when we went to bed, and the greenhouse plants are frozen!'[13] Without waiting for her to cover her head 'in the dim of dawn', they went out together to see the dead plants. Everything there looked 'strange, ghostly, unreal'. The whole week at St. Juliot now seemed unreal, and Hardy began to think that there was little chance of his ever seeing E. L. G. again. 'Their differing habits and . . . contrasting positions': 'Farewell!' he said, 'I soon must be gone!'

> Even then, the scale might have been turned
> Against love by a feather,
> But crimson one cheek of hers burned
> When we came in together.[14]

Not satisfied with merely kissing her cheek, he kissed her lips too — at least 'in fancy, as I came away in the morning glow'. So he wrote, long after, in 'Two Lips'. 'I kissed them through the glass of her picture-frame.'

On the train-ride back to Bockhampton, Hardy had abundant time to think over what had happened to him. For

> at waning of this week
> Broke a new life on me.[15]

He never forgot what a few days' experience could do in a man's life, and in 'A Week' he made poetic harvest of his discovery. In this poem

> On Wednesday I did not opine
> Your life would ever be one with mine.

But by the time the week was over, he could confess :

> On Sunday night I longed for thee,
> Without whom life were waste to me ! [16]

Upon his return to the cottage at Higher Bockhampton, he could not long conceal from the observant eyes of his father and mother, or doubtless from his sisters, that something unusual had happened to him. They said nothing, but they noticed — and 'surmised'.

> When I came from Lyonnesse
> With magic in my eyes,
> All marked with mute surmise
> My radiance rare and fathomless,
> When I came back from Lyonnesse
> With magic in my eyes ! [17]

III

'STARRY THOUGHTS'

In the weeks that followed Hardy's return to Dorset, he found his thoughts constantly revolving to that isolated Cornish spot where

> Within walls of weathered stone
> Far away . . .
> Lives a Sweet : no merchants meet,
> No man barters, no man sells
> Where she dwells.[1]

He couldn't get the vision of that lady in brown out of his mind. 'She was so living', he used to say.[2] In the poem 'Ditty' he called her 'a Sweet', not a Beauty. 'Though her features were not regular, her complexion . . . was perfect . . . her figure and movement graceful, and her corn-coloured hair abundant in its coils.'[2] In June he found himself thinking 'of that kiss . . . by the strawberry-tree'.[3] It was, for him then, and for his memories thereof long afterwards, a time of 'freshness, fairness, fulness, fineness'.[3]

> Show me again the time
> When in the Junetide's prime . . .
> Love lured life on.[3]

On 8 August 1870 Hardy again left for Cornwall. Upon his arrival at St. Juliot, he found the 'young lady in brown', of the previous March, now 'metamorphosed into a young lady in summer blue, which suited her fair complexion far better ; and the visit was a most happy one'.[4] He spent most of August in Cornwall. 'Often we walked to Boscastle Harbour down the beautiful

Valency Valley, where we had to jump over stones . . . to come out on great wide spaces . . . with a sparkling little brook . . . in which we once lost a tiny picnic tumbler, and there it is to this day no doubt.' So Emma reported. We know the date when this episode took place, for Hardy drew a sketch of Emma searching for the lost tumbler, and dated his sketch : 19 August 1870.[5] Later, he wrote a poem about it, 'Under the Waterfall', in which he imagines Emma Gifford telling the story of the loss :

> We placed our basket of fruit and wine
> By the runlet's rim, where we sat to dine ;
> And when we had drunk from the glass together,
> Arched by the oak-copse from the weather,
> I held the vessel to rinse in the fall,
> Where it slipped, and sank, and was past recall.
> . . . There the glass still is.[6]

Many years later, he came back to the site of that summer picnic, and found that he could

> scan and trace
> The forsaken place
> Quite readily,

and he subsequently wrote yet another poem about it — 'Where the Picnic Was'.[7]

Three days later, Hardy and Emma Gifford went again to Beeny Cliff. There, once more, Hardy sketched the scene and dated his sketch : 22 August 1870. It began to rain. Emma sat down and drew her cape around her, but Hardy kept on sketching. His picture (reproduced on page 82 of *Some Recollections*, by Emma Hardy) shows how accurately he described the scene, the weather, and his companion, in his poem 'The Figure in the Scene' :

> It pleased her to step in front and sit
> Where the craggèd slope was green,

While I stood back that I might pencil it
With her amid the scene ;
Till it gloomed and rained ;
But I kept on . . .[8]

A second poem, 'Why Did I Sketch', makes use of this
same episode, when he had stood to

sketch an upland green
And put the figure in
Of one on the spot with me.[9]

Neither poem is of great importance as literature, but
together they serve to fill in the gaps in the biography
of the poet.

It was perhaps this same cold and gloomy rain of
22 August that led Emma Lavinia Gifford to remark

'It never looks like summer here
On Beeny by the sea.'

Forty-three years later, Hardy completed the quatrain :

But though she saw its look as drear,
Summer it seemed to me.[10]

Emma's *Recollections* of that August include the statement that 'sometimes we . . . drove to . . . Bossiney
. . . and other places on the coast'. Hardy's poem
'Self-Unconscious' was composed 'near Bossiney' — or
at least was inspired by the thoughts that came to him,
many years later, when he was revisiting this spot to
which he and E. L. G. had driven together. With the
wisdom of old age he could look back to the Bossiney
visit of 1870 and opine that

it would have been good
Could he then have stood
At a clear-eyed distance, and conned the whole,[11]

but under the spell of his Cornish romance he saw little
beyond the present. 'The visit was a most happy one.'

On his return to Bockhampton, he often sat down to his desk to write, but instead found himself mooning about Emma.

> And I have wasted another day.
> But wasted — *wasted*, do I say ?
> Is it a waste to have imaged one
> Beyond the hills there, who, anon,
>   My great deeds done,
>   Will be mine alway ? [12]

Letters went back and forth between Dorchester (*i.e.* Bockhampton) and St. Juliot ; and gradually, one by one, 'the grey gaunt days dividing us twain', and the 'slow blank months' of the winter of 1870–71 passed. In May 1871 there was another visit to Cornwall. Hardy was now almost thirty-one years old, but his desire to marry Miss Gifford was overshadowed by the thought that he had not, thus far, made a real success of anything. His feeling of discouragement is quite understandable. Nor is there any cause for surprise in our discovering that his discouragement has left its trail in a sonnet which he wrote shortly before seeing Miss Gifford again :

> knowing . . . what is now about to be . . .
> I read beyond it my despondency
> When more dividing months shall take its place. [13]

Hardy had, of course, reason enough to despond. He could write about 'my great deeds done' — meaning, of course, 'when my as-yet-unaccomplished but hoped-for great deeds shall have been done' — but he had not, as yet, done much more than dream about them. In writing to Miss Gifford, he had made no secret of the fact that his past efforts did not encourage rosy thoughts of the future. He had gone up to London shortly before his twenty-second birthday, and had found employment as an architect. Within a year, he had been awarded two professional prizes — one by the Royal Institute of British Architects, the other by the Architectural Association — but neither award had led to anything more. Five years in the big city brought him thereafter nothing but discouragement. He had tried his hand at writing verses and had sent his poetry to various editors, but it invariably came back. Not a single poem was accepted. In the world of aspiring architects, Hardy had decided, after five years of watching how social 'contacts' and clever talk can take precedence over merit, that he had had enough of London. He returned to Dorset and there tried his hand at writing novels. He had to confess to Miss Gifford, however, that his first attempt at fiction had been turned down by three publishers, and that his second had been rejected by Alexander Macmillan. And in order to get this second novel (called *Desperate Remedies*) into print, Hardy had taken the desperate step of hazarding seventy-five pounds, a large part of his savings, in order to induce Tinsley Brothers to publish it. The novel appeared at the end of March 1871, a little more than a month before Hardy made his next visit to St. Juliot.

A third trip followed in the autumn. Hardy spent much of October at the rectory, but he cannot have concealed from E. L. G. the uncertainty of his prospects. In this time of discouragement, Miss Gifford proved to be more than an able horsewoman 'with bright hair flapping free', more than an accomplished musician who could sing sentimental songs and play duets with her sister, more than a vivacious girl

> With cheeks whose airy flush outbid
> Fresh fruit in bloom,

and more than an artist who could sketch and do watercolours. She lent a sympathetic ear to Hardy's discussion of his chance of literary success. She smiled upon his proposal to turn his back upon the architect's draughting-board and encouraged him to persevere in his efforts to write fiction. She offered to copy manuscript for him. She discussed incidents and ideas that he could perhaps use in his plots. In short, she did what no other woman of his acquaintance had as yet been able to do with him and for him : she encouraged him in the determined pursuit of what interested him most — literary composition. His 'great deeds' were to be done by writing — not by building manor-houses or restoring old churches. Nor was Hardy unaware of the significant part that her encouragement played in rendering him immune to the chilling blasts that blew from London :

> In the seventies I was bearing in my breast,
> > Penned tight,
> Certain starry thoughts that threw a magic light
> On the worktimes and the soundless hours of rest. . . .
>
> In the seventies those who met me did not know
> > Of the vision
> That immuned me from the chillings of misprision
> And the damps that choked my goings to and fro
> In the seventies ; yea, those nodders did not know
> > Of the vision.[14]

With the encouragement of Miss Gifford, Hardy did persevere with his writing. *Desperate Remedies* was followed by the composition of *Under the Greenwood Tree*, and this novel was published in June 1872. By the time Hardy made his August 1872 visit to St. Juliot, he could report that he had received thirty pounds for the copyright in this latter novel. Slight though this 'success' may seem — slight indeed in comparison with Hardy's major successes in the years to come — he and Emma were sufficiently encouraged by this improvement in the literary weather to do what they had, apparently, not done up to this time. They decided to let Miss Gifford's father know of their intentions. Hardy was now thirty-two, Emma was thirty-one. They did not *have* to obtain paternal consent to their marriage. But it was customary to ask for it ; besides, Emma had a high regard for her father. So they 'rose and went'.

Emma's father was a retired solicitor living at Bodmin, in Cornwall. His name was John Attersoll Gifford. He was the elder brother of the Reverend Doctor Edwin Hamilton Gifford, Canon of Worcester Cathedral. In Emma Gifford's girlhood the family had lived in Plymouth. There she had been born in 1840, and there she had spent the first eighteen years of her life. 'My home', she later reminisced, 'was a most intellectual one and not only so but one of exquisite home-training and refinement — alas [so she wrote in 1911] the difference the loss of these amenities and gentlenesses has made to me !'

By 1872, however, the Giffords had moved from Plymouth to Bodmin, because, 'when my dear Grandmamma died . . . in 1859, we had to retrench on account of her income being divided, and it was decided to go to Cornwall. . . . Cornwall was very strange at first, after we had had to leave our very pleasant home [in Plymouth].' [15]

'After we had been a few years in Bodmin, my sister, on account of the dullness and necessity of earning something, started off as a governess . . . but after six months returned home. . . . My sister married, as his second wife, the Reverend Cadell Holder . . . a man older than herself by many years. . . . They were married from our house . . . and I went with them to St. Juliot Rectory. . . .' [16]

There is no evidence in Emma Hardy's *Recollections*

that, after this departure from the paternal roof, she ever resided there again. She held her father in high repute, however, and in 1911 described him as 'altogether a well-read man with a good memory for literary anecdotes . . . ; he was fond particularly of writing and speaking Latin ; his love of Shakespeare was great he constantly quoted' [sic].[17]

Emma Gifford now, in 1872, decided that the time had come to introduce Thomas Hardy to her father and to acquaint him with their intentions. St. Juliot was within easy distance of Bodmin. They went. To her consternation, her father not only expressed disapproval of the marriage, but later denounced Hardy in violent language as 'that base churl who has presumed to wish to marry into my family'.

The young lovers never got over that harsh rebuff. Emma had enough of her father's pride of class — 'my home was one of exquisite refinement' — to understand (and even to sympathize with) his feeling that Hardy was a crude upstart ; but she also had enough loyalty to her 'chosen one' (as she called him) to sense what a painful, wound had been given to Hardy's self-respect. Later on, he was to versify her thoughts for her. In 'I Rose and Went to Rou'tor Town' Hardy did what he often enjoyed doing in other poems : he represented Emma as the speaker — 'she, alone'. The last stanza reads :

> The evil wrought at Rou'tor Town
>   On him I'd loved so true
>   I cannot tell anew :
> But nought can quench, but nought can drown
> The evil wrought at Rou'tor Town
>   On him I'd loved so true ![18]

The reader will notice that, in writing this poem, Hardy left the details and identities vague ; but he chose for his poem exactly the same stanzaic form he had used in his ecstatic 'When I Set Out for Lyonnesse'. In the one, *he* spoke ; in the other, *she* spoke. But how tragic the change in tone !

While they were still under the cloud of this paternal denunciation, Hardy and Emma walked out from Bodmin on the road to Lanivet. She became tired, and when they came to 'a stunted handpost' on the road, they stopped to rest.

> She leant back, being so weary, against its stem,
>   And laid her arms on its own . . .
> Her white-clothed form . . .
>   Made her look as one crucified. . . .
>
>   . . . hurriedly 'Don't,' I cried.
> I do not think she heard. . . .
>
> 'I am rested now.—Something strange came into my head,
>   I wish I had not leant so !'
>
> . . . wordless we moved onward . . . till she said. . . .
>   '. . . If no one is bodily crucified now,
>   In spirit one may be !'
>
> And we dragged on and on, while we seemed to see
>   In the running of Time's far glass
> Her crucified, as she had wondered if she might be
>   Some day.—Alas, alas ! [19]

Depressed, they returned to St. Juliot, and there (in August 1872) Hardy completed the first instalment of *A Pair of Blue Eyes* which Tinsley began to serialize in the September issue of his magazine. Hardy and Emma were able to take some consolation in the fact that the publisher agreed to pay the author two hundred pounds for this novel, even before Hardy had finished writing it. In the Preface which he wrote for this, his fourth fictional work, Hardy remarked : 'The attempt made here is to trace the influence of character on circumstances. The conduct pursued . . . by a young girl supplies the foundation on which I have built this book.'

Later on, Hardy discarded this preface and in 1895 wrote a wholly new one. In 1872, however, it is important to look over his shoulder and see him at work in the rectory at St. Juliot, for we know who the 'young girl' was ; and when we come to Chapter XXII, in which the sea moans below 'the Cliff without a Name', *we* know what the actual name of that cliff is, for we have twice before been to Beeny in the company of Hardy and E. L. G.

After the painful trip to the country 'near Lanivet', the ex-architect and his sweetheart never went back there. They varied their meetings at St. Juliot with what Emma called 'two pleasant changes' of scene — one in Bath and one in London. In June and July 1873 Hardy spent ten days at Bath, while Miss Gifford was the guest there of a Miss d'Arville, 'a delightful old lady'. Hardy escorted Miss Gifford to Clifton, to Chepstow, and up the river Wye to Tintern Abbey. The London visit, when Emma 'went as country cousin to my brother in London', was apparently not as successful and happy as the Bath sojourn had been. She arrived 'with a travel-tired smile' — the railway trip up from Cornwall was a long one — and on her arrival at the station, where Hardy stood 'mid murks of night . . . to await her', she seemed

> Half scared by scene so strange
> . . . outworn by mile on mile [20]

of travel. However, 'Love, I am here ! I am with you !' she exclaimed, and the fatigue of the long journey was soon forgotten.

Before the end of the year 1873 there was another meeting at St. Juliot. Once again, on 'a day of latter summer, hot and dry', the two paid a visit to the coast. There, near 'a jutting height . . . with a margin of blue sea' — obviously Beeny Cliff again — Emma, 'calmly quite . . . unfolded what would happen by and by'. Her dire predictions coloured all his later associations with the place.

> So, the map revives her words, the spot, the time,
> And the thing we found we had to face before the next
>   year's prime ;
>   The charted coast stares bright,
> And its episode comes back in pantomime.[21]

The thing they had to face was the risk of marriage with no more financial security than Hardy's pen was able to provide, and with parental disapproval lowering in the background. Both lovers knew that Mr. Gifford would never forgive them if they married. Helen Catherine (Emma's sister) had been married from her father's house. Emma knew that if she were to wed Thomas Hardy it would have to be done elsewhere. She eventually decided to go once again 'as country cousin to my brother in London'.

The year 1874 was the year of decision. The *Cornhill* began serializing *Far from the Madding Crowd* in January. Reviewers were immediately enthusiastic. In February Hardy's identity as the author of the new novel was disclosed, and the future looked bright. The *Cornhill* paid well, and before many days had passed, Hardy learned that there would be additional money coming to him from America. Before the year 1874 was over, *Far from the Madding Crowd* had been published five times in the United States. Hardy and Miss Gifford decided to act.

On 17 September 1874 they appeared at St. Peter's

Church in Elgin Avenue, Paddington, London, and there her uncle, Dr. E. Hamilton Gifford, Canon of Worcester Cathedral, married them. They went off to France, to spend a brief honeymoon in Rouen and Paris, and while they were away, thousands of people in England were reading the September issue of the *Cornhill* magazine in which Chapter XLI of *Far from the Madding Crowd* appeared. One would like to know what Mrs. Hardy's comment on that chapter was. The dialogue between Bathsheba and her newly-acquired husband, Francis Troy, runs thus :

'Bathsheba . . . don't go too far, or you may have cause to regret something.'
'I do that already,' she said.
'What do you regret ?'
'That my romance has come to an end.'
'All romances end at marriage.'
'I wish you wouldn't talk like that. You grieve me to my soul.'

At the end of the honeymoon in France, Thomas and Emma Hardy returned to England and settled down, for the winter of 1874–75, in lodgings at St. David's, Hook Road, Surbiton, south of Kingston. Here they looked across the river Thames to Hampton Court Park.

IV

THE YELLOWING LEAF

AT Surbiton, Hardy set about writing his next novel, *The Hand of Ethelberta*. In the forty-third chapter of this story the heroine remarks :

> I have seen marriages where happiness might have been said to be ensured, and they have been all sadness afterwards; and I have seen those in which the prospect was black as night, and they have led on to a time of sweetness and comfort. And I have seen marriages neither joyful nor sorry, that have become either as accident forced them to become, the persons having no voice in it at all.

Since it was Hardy himself who made Ethelberta speak thus, we may well wonder in which one of the three categories he would have placed his own marriage.

As far as his poetry of later years supplies any evidence, we must conclude that Hardy's marriage was 'neither joyful nor sorry', or — better still — it was both joyful *and* sorry, though not for the reason assigned by Ethelberta. She had declared that 'accident' — Hardy's 'crass casualty' — sometimes decided the matter, 'the persons having no voice in it at all'. In Hardy's case, the persons did have a voice in it, and both parties used their voices.

The newly married couple lived quietly at Surbiton — 'no diners out were we' — but they did accept one invitation to a house 'where almost strangers were we'. There one of 'Lavine's' (*i.e.* Emma Lavinia's) curious superstitions cast 'a gloom over the dinner'. There were thirteen at the table. In a shadow cast on 'a distant screen' Mrs. Hardy saw her 'own body lying'. The 'new bride' saw her 'own corpse' stretched out. Of course Hardy himself was not wholly free from superstitions — he would never allow himself to be weighed because that would bring bad luck! — but he now discovered in his bride a morbid streak of what she was later to call her 'mysticism', to which he was, fortunately, less addicted.[1]

In the spring of 1875 the Hardys moved to Bournemouth for a brief stay, and there, on a rainy day in mid-July, they got on each other's nerves. 'We were irked by the scene, by our own selves.'[2] Later on, he came to recognize that there had been blindness on *both* sides :

> . . . I did not know, nor did she infer
> How much there was to read and guess
> By her in me, and to see and crown
> By me in her.[2]

But at the moment, 'that July time, when the rain came down', there was only one thing certain : 'great was the waste'.[2] Hardy's marriage was already proving to have its sorrowful, as well as its joyful, aspect. The worst of it was that he 'did not know'. She was not frank with him, nor he with her. Their silence only made matters worse. A rift had developed — minor at first, but one that was destined to grow. In 'The Rift' he confesses :

> So sank I from my high sublime !
> And never I knew or guessed my crime.[3]

The Hardys shortly moved to near-by Swanage, and there, on the shore of the English Channel, *The Hand of Ethelberta* was finished. While there, they experienced another stormy day ; but, this time, it was only the weather that was stormy : joy rather than wasteful sorrow characterized their mood when 'there we two stood, hands clasped, I and she!'[4]

In March 1876 they moved again, this time to Yeovil ;

and after a May vacation-trip to Holland and the Rhine, they settled, in July, at Sturminster Newton. Here, for the first time, they had a house all to themselves — one which they had to furnish — and here they spent two years : 'our happiest time' Hardy later called it (*Early Life*, p. 156). The Bournemouth 'rift' was forgotten — momentarily at least — and in 'A Two-Years' Idyll' Hardy recalled with great pleasure 'those two seasons' when he was engaged in writing *The Return of the Native*.[5] At that time, however, he was unaware — as later experience was to make him aware — of the fact that he was blind to some aspects of his stay at Sturminster Newton, idyllic though it was. He noticed lots of *little* things — 'the river gleam', the 'moor-hen', the 'kingcups' — but

> . . . never I turned my head, alack,
> To see the more behind my back.[6]

And in 'The Musical Box' he is even more explicit about the fact that he 'did not hear [and] did not see'. As he would come back from a walk 'by Stourside Mill', Emma would 'laugh a hailing as she scanned him in the gloom', but the poet ends his lines by expressing his belated and now-futile regret : 'I did not see'.[7] Emma did more than 'scan him in the gloom' : she copied manuscript for Hardy, and a number of the pages of the final 'printer's copy' manuscript of *The Return of the Native* are in her hand, not his.

When the two-years' idyll came to an end, Hardy and his wife moved to Upper Tooting (south-west London), and there they soon had reason to think

> There is some hid dread afoot
> That we cannot trace.[8]

Whatever may have been the immediate cause of their fears, there was one aspect of their relationship which, though perhaps obscure to them, is clear enough to us. We have had the benefit of a century-long documentation of their lives. The class-consciousness which Emma had unwittingly learned from her father, and the lack of frankness between the novelist and his wife, when they stumbled upon points of difference in their backgrounds and habits, these sources of friction were still there ; but these were minor matters when set beside the fundamental disagreement of the Hardys on religious matters. In the days of his courtship, Hardy doubtless refrained from making clear to Emma how totally he had come to reject all the religious teachings on which she had been brought up. He had, it is true, attended church as a boy, both at Stinsford and in Dorchester ; he had at one time taught a Sunday school class in the Stinsford church, and as a youth had contemplated the possibility of taking holy orders. But Darwin and John Stuart Mill and Herbert Spencer had rendered such a future impossible for Hardy ; before he was twenty, he had lost all belief in Christian dogma. Like Angel Clare in *Tess*, he had 'liberated his mind from the untenable redemptive theolatry' of the Established Church. Emma, on the other hand, had not only grown up with deeply rooted orthodox views but continued to hold tenaciously to them. In Plymouth and, later, at St. Juliot, she had been not only a regular attendant at church — Hardy had been *that* — but also an unquestioning acceptor of the Faith. When she met Hardy, his familiarity with the church services, his fondness for the church music, his thoroughgoing acquaintance with the Bible, both in English and in Greek, all served to conceal from her the fact that — intellectually — their views were poles asunder. After their marriage, she soon discovered his unwillingness to attend church with her. In novel after novel, she discovered his possession of views she not only could not agree with, but to which she was radically opposed. The fact that the expression of these views in the novels was assigned to one character or another could not, in the long run, conceal from her the fact that she had married a husband who had no belief in an ordered universe, in a Divine Plan, or in a loving and beneficent Providence. Her pronouncements of belief in the Virgin Birth, in vicarious atonement, in a future life, in eternal salvation, fell upon deaf ears when she addressed Thomas Hardy. When she read in *Far from the Madding Crowd* that 'your lot is your lot and Scripture is nothing', or in *The Return of the Native* that your lot is determined by whim and caprice, 'the fault of some indistinct colossal Prince of the World' rather than the loving dispensation of an all-wise Father in Heaven, she was revolted ; nor were her feelings helped by reading in *The Return of the Native* about 'sinking into the mire of marriage'. Who was this strange husband she had married, anyway ? We recall Hardy's words about her — that she did not infer 'how much there was to read and guess by her' in him — how true that was ! Though not in the way that he meant it !

Meanwhile Emma continued the manuscript-copying which she had begun at Sturminster Newton. Hardy was, like many other authors, a writer who revised and revised and revised, until eventually his papers approached illegibility. Then Emma was called upon to make a clean copy. The manuscript of *The Trumpet-Major* shows that she did for this novel, at Upper Tooting, the same sort of writing a 'fair copy' that she had done with *The Return of the Native* at Sturminster Newton.

Hardy's 'some hid dread afoot' soon took on an unexpected and painful form : in 1880 he became seriously ill, and for months had to lie in bed with his feet propped up higher than his head. In this way an internal haemorrhage was, eventually, successfully combated ; but during the long period of his illness, Mrs. Hardy had not only to devote herself to bedside nursing, but had to play amanuensis as well. For Hardy had contracted to supply fiction which was as yet unwritten ; and, to earn their living, to keep the wolf from the door, and to meet the doctor's bills, he strove valiantly to live up to the terms of his contract. While playing nurse, Mrs. Hardy had to take down the text of *A Laodicean* at his dictation. Her devoted service in these varied capacities has, so far as I know, left no trace in any poem written by him. His lines

> . . . never I turned my head, alack,
> To see the more behind my back

refer to his Sturminster Newton idyll and not to his illness and convalescence in London, but there too he failed to turn his head to see. From what is absent in his poems, we learn about one side of his nature that certainly brought very little joy to Emma Hardy's heart.

Upon his recovery, the Hardys moved to Wimborne, and there *Two on a Tower* was written. The manuscript of this novel shows under what pressure it was composed. As Hardy wrote, his pages soon became particularly messy : the manuscript is filled with corrections, suppressions, additions, inversions, and transpositions. As a result, Emma's copying had to be more extensive as well as more meticulous than it had been with previous novels. Moreover, since this story was to be serialized exclusively in an American magazine, Hardy decided that he would like to have a second copy, 'to guard against accidental loss', as he explained to the editor of the *Atlantic Monthly*, telling him that 'a duplicate will follow by the next mail'. Emma of course had to help make this duplicate copy.

Dozens of pages of the manuscript are in her hand. She also wrote some of the business letters dealing with this publication — letters in which Hardy's part of the writing was confined to his signature. In the autumn of 1883 they moved again, this time to Dorchester, where they took up residence in an old house with only one window in front, a window which looked out into Gaol Lane. The house stood in Shire Hall Lane, 'one of the little-used alleys of the town'. Here they were near the doorway, 'arched and old', which Hardy was shortly to describe in the twenty-first chapter of *The Mayor of Casterbridge* :

> The keystone of the arch was a mask. Originally the mask had exhibited a comic leer, but generations of Casterbridge boys had thrown stones at the mask, aiming at its open mouth, and the blows thereon had chipped off the lips and jaws as if they had been eaten away by disease. The appearance was so ghastly by the weak lamp glimmer that she could not bear to look at it.

The 'she' of this description is, of course, Elizabeth-Jane ; but one wonders whether her reaction to this ghastly appearance was suggested to the author's mind by Emma Hardy's similar revulsion on first seeing the leering mask near her new 'home'. In any case, there, in the 'little-used alley', so old and familiar to Hardy, so new and unattractive to his wife, the two of them were living when their tenth wedding anniversary arrived on 17 September 1884. No poem written by Hardy celebrated that occasion.

V

'OUR OWN NEW-BUILDED DOOR'

SHORTLY after Mr. and Mrs. Thomas Hardy settled in
Shire Hall Lane in Dorchester, he again donned the architect's rôle which he had discarded ten years previously.
Hardy now designed a house — his first (and last) such
design. It was to be his own residence. He acquired a
small plot of land a mile outside of Dorchester on the
road to Wareham, and there, in the course of eighteen
months (1883–85), the dwelling to be known as Max
Gate arose. The Hardys moved in on 29 June 1885. The
house is still standing, and many a twentieth-century
visitor to it has had occasion to question Hardy's abilities
as an architect. In general design, in plumbing, in light,
and convenience, the house has impressed many persons
as falling far short of modern standards for comfortable
living ; and some of Hardy's later poems suggest that
Emma was not slow in expressing her dissatisfaction with
the new dwelling.

> 'The house is bleak and cold,
>   Built so new for me,'[1]

she is quoted as having said. He promised to plant trees

> As a screen . . .
> Both from winds, and eyes that tease,[1]

but he was so slow in doing so that the 'grove' mentioned
in one line of the poem was not full grown until after

her death ! In 'The Tree and the Lady', Hardy repre-
sents one of the trees at Max Gate as the disappointed
speaker :

> I have done all I could
> For that lady I knew ! . . .
> At the mirth-time of May
> . . . my shadow first lured her
> . . . Much did I treasure her
> During those days she had nothing to pleasure her ;
> . . . now, . . .
> Gone is she, scorning my bough ! [2]

But the Tree is not the only cynical speaker on this
subject of the new house. In 'Fetching Her' Hardy
imagines one of his friends speaking to him about his
folly in bringing a Cornish bride 'unto your own new-
builded door' in Dorset :

> You sought her on her surfy shore,
> To fetch her thence away. . . .
> — But time is prompt to expugn
> Such magic-minted conjurings :
> The brought breeze fainted soon. [3]

As we read the poem, we are left with the wistful uncertainty of a man who is wondering whether he might not
have been happier if he

> had not pulled this flower
> And set it in an alien bower
> But left it where it grew. [3]

Four-score years have passed since Hardy designed his
new home, and the reader of his poems is now in a
favoured position for surmising at least one of the reasons
why 'the brought breeze fainted soon'. A few weeks
before moving into Max Gate, Hardy left Mrs. Hardy in
the Shire Hall Lane lodgings and went off to Devon to
spend a few days as the house-guest of Lord and Lady

Portsmouth. True, Mrs. Hardy had been invited to accompany him; but when illness, or indisposition, or some other reason, led her to stay at home, he went without her. True, he wrote to her immediately upon his arrival at Eggesford House, Wembworthy, Devon,[4] telling her all about the bevy of ladies, old and young, by whom he found himself surrounded, but it was quite obvious that he was enjoying himself there much more than he would have if he had remained in Shire Hall Lane.

By this date Emma Hardy knew her husband well enough to realize that he was quite susceptible to feminine attractions. Hardy liked the attention society ladies gave him and he responded to their flattery. These attentions to the popular novelist had begun in London, and by now — 1885 — Hardy was acquainted with a long list of ladies, duchesses, marchionesses, countesses, and other 'noble dames'. His talk and his letters, and (we can now add) his private notes, began to be increasingly full of these names.

> Lady Portsmouth's black brocaded silk gown fitted her well. Lady Yarborough was 'very rich and very pretty'. Lady Stracey 'looked remarkably well'. Lady P—— was 'the most beautiful woman there'. Miss—— was a 'handsome girl' with a 'cruel small mouth'. Mrs. Jeune 'looked handsome'. Mrs. T—— 'and her great eyes' was 'the most beautiful woman present'. Mrs. Thornycraft's mouth recalled an Elizabethan poem. Mrs. R. C. and Mrs. A. G. were 'a pair of beauties'; the latter, 'with her violet eyes, was the more seductive'. [5]

No wonder Mrs. Hardy, brooding near the leering mask, began to feel that the husband with whom she had fallen in love in Cornwall and whom she had nursed so devotedly back to health in London was being spoiled. Flattery from the duchesses was going to his head. No wonder Emma Hardy later blurted out to T. P. O'Connor that her husband was really 'very vain and very selfish. And these women that he meets in London society only increase these things. They are the poison ; I am the antidote.' [6] Unfortunately, in trying to apply the antidote to the situation at Max Gate, Mrs. Hardy poisoned herself. The breeze brought from Cornwall 'fainted soon'.

Instead of making of the new home a dwelling where Hardy would like to abide, she succeeded in making it a place from which he was often glad to escape. He had once found London 'crushes' unrewarding and unattractive, but now he was, with increasing frequency, willing to follow Robert Browning's notoriously sociable example. Hardy was seen more and more frequently at London dinner-tables, at London tea-tables, in London theatres, in London club-rooms. Curiously enough, when he was in Dorchester, Hardy came to rely more than ever on his wife for help in making a clean manuscript. A hundred and more leaves of *The Woodlanders* — written in 1886–87 — are in Emma's hand. The manuscript of *Tess*, begun in 1888, also shows the marks of her copying, and the manuscript of some of the *Noble Dames* (1889) is partly in her hand. When Hardy sent the manuscript of 'The Doctor's Legend' to Bliss Carman for publication in *The Independent* (New York, 26 March 1891), that manuscript was almost entirely in Mrs. Hardy's handwriting. She was a busy woman in these years, and her services as amanuensis have never been given the recognition they deserve.

At the Max Gate dinner-table, however, the periods of silence were growing and the topics on which the Hardys did not talk were obviously increasing in number. There was, moreover, one new subject on which the novelist and his wife apparently came to a tacit agreement soon after the move into Max Gate. Hardy's first novel, unpublished, had been called 'The Poor Man and the Lady'. Now that the Poor Man had become a comfortably well-to-do man, able to build himself a house, it was understood that the Lady would have nothing to do with the Poor Man's family. *He* could go to see the dwellers in the cottage at Higher Bockhampton, but he would go alone. Hardy made weekly visits to call on his parents, but there is no record of Mrs. Emma Hardy's having ever invited them to Max Gate. Hardy's sisters, Mary and Kate, continued to reside only three miles away, but Emma never invited them to call. Hardy's brother Henry was sometimes made use of : when Emma and her husband went to London for an extended stay during the 'season', Henry Hardy could be called upon to pay the gardener at Max Gate, or he could be asked to help with odd jobs of carpentering ; but that was all.

Thus, in all these years while the trees at Max Gate were pushing their roots down into the Dorset soil, the poison and the antidote were doing their insidious work inside the house. Hardy's thoughts were, naturally enough, on his growing fame as a successful author — he now had ten novels to his credit — and he found it pleasant to talk with people in London who read his books. Emma's resentful thoughts were on the way 'these women in London society' were spoiling her husband. The attention of both was directed Londonwards ; neither had time to give much thought to the elderly couple — Hardy's parents — at Higher Bockhampton. And then, on 20 July 1892, Hardy's father died. The old master-mason would play his violin no more.

The loss of his father resulted in Hardy's coming to feel — one wonders whether it was the first time he had

had that feeling — that he really did not know himself very well. He wrote a revealing poem, called 'The Self-Unseeing', in which he pictured his parents in the Bockhampton cottage, and himself, 'childlike', looking the other way. The poem was published ten years later, at which time Hardy proposed calling the volume in which it appeared *Poems of Feeling*, but this title he later decided not to use. Emma's part in the poem is confined to the word 'we' in the last line ; but, since she is a vital part of Hardy's reason for 'looking away', the poem is included in the present volume. Hardy wrote :

> She sat here in her chair,
>   Smiling into the fire ;
> He who played stood there,
>   Bowing it higher and higher.
>
> Childlike, I danced in a dream ;
>   Blessings emblazoned that day ;
> Everything glowed with a gleam ;
>   Yet we were looking away ! [7]

Alas for the blessing-emblazoned but unseeing author ! Before the winds of another twelve months had passed over the trees at Max Gate, their owner was looking farther away than ever.

VI
'OUR DEEP DIVISION'

THE funeral of Hardy's father provides a biographical
milestone which is useful for our study in a variety of
ways. To begin with, that funeral upset a plan which
Hardy had been contemplating for a trip to Ireland. To
explain this statement we must embark upon a somewhat
complicated retrospect.

Among the people whom the novelist had met in
London was Richard Monckton Milnes, the first Lord
Houghton. In June 1883 Hardy was a guest at a luncheon
given by the baron, and he may have met Lord Houghton's
daughter Florence at this (or at some subsequent) time.
In 1882, when she was twenty-seven, Florence Milnes
had married a young army officer, Lieutenant Arthur H.
Henniker. Three years later, Mrs. Henniker's father died;
and when her younger brother, the second Baron Hough-
ton, was appointed Lord-Lieutenant of Ireland, Mrs.
Henniker went to Dublin to serve as his hostess at the
Viceregal Lodge while her husband was absent from
England on active duty with the British army. Florence
Henniker had literary ambitions, and just at the time when
Hardy's *Tess* was appearing, she turned novelist, publish-
ing *Sir George* in 1891, *Bid Me Good-bye* in 1892, and
Foiled in 1893. In 1892 Mrs. Henniker invited the Hardys
to visit her and her brother in Dublin. Hardy cannot have
pretended to having the slightest interest in Ireland, but an
invitation from an attractive woman was a different matter.
The invitation was accepted. The illness, however, and

then the death, of Hardy's father forced a postponement of the trip to Dublin.

It was while Hardy was still under the cloud of this bereavement that he penned his 'Preface to the Fifth Edition' of *Tess*, dating it July 1892. In it he acknowledged 'the responsive spirit in which *Tess of the d'Urbervilles* has been received by the readers of England and America', and then he added (in words to which the reader will wish to give careful heed) : 'For this responsiveness I cannot refrain from expressing my thanks ; and my regret is that, in a world where one so often hungers in vain for friendship . . . I shall never meet in person these appreciative readers, male and female, and shake them by the hand.'

A few days after the funeral for Hardy's father, when the novelist was doubtless feeling more painfully than ever that he was living 'in a world where one so often hungers in vain for friendship', he was surprised by receiving a call from two of his most 'appreciative readers . . . female' in America, the Misses Rebekah and Catharine Owen of New York City. These sisters not only called at Max Gate but also made so instant and pleasing an impression upon the novelist that three years later he put them both into the preface of a new edition of *The Mayor of Casterbridge*, in which he described them as 'some good judges across the Atlantic'. [1]

Mrs. Hardy, too, was struck with the New York ladies. She called on them five days later and invited them to tea at Max Gate. When they went on the appointed day (Friday, 12 August 1892), they found Hardy busily occupied with a lady whom he introduced, with a twinkle in his eye, merely as Tess. The Owen sisters learned later that she was Miss Teresa Charlotte Fetherstonhaugh-Frampton, great-great-great-granddaughter of

Betty, First Countess of Wessex (the first of Hardy's *Noble Dames*). No report of the conversation of that day has come down to us, but shortly afterwards Mrs. Hardy hurried off to Bournemouth.

A few years later, when (as we shall see shortly) a young bride consulted Mrs. Hardy as to what was the best thing for the wife of a literary man to do when a domestic crisis occurred, Emma Hardy replied : 'Keeping separate a good deal is a wise plan in crises'. Whether her abrupt dashing off to Bournemouth in August 1892 was the result of a 'crisis' at Max Gate, we have now no sure way of knowing ; but on 20 August Mrs. Hardy came dashing back again and then wrote to Rebekah Owen : 'I returned from Bournemouth on Saturday, as the place was in a congested state with tourists and excursionists. I hope to drive out this afternoon, and wonder whether you would care to join me.' In this way she was able to enjoy the good judges from across the Atlantic all by herself, without having to share them with her partner at Max Gate.

Mrs. Hardy's frequent trips with hired conveyances — a 'pony-carriage' — 'hired from the Antelope' (hotel at Dorchester) — have had one advantage for posterity. Miss Owen recorded some of Emma's remarks, and on one occasion photographed her. We therefore know what Mrs. Hardy looked like on 18 September 1892.[2] As for her remarks, they give us an insight into her critical powers. Regarding *The Hand of Ethelberta* : 'I never liked that novel : too much about servants in it'. Of *Tess of the d'Urbervilles* : 'We called her Rose Mary Troublefield so long that it is hard now to think of her as Tess'. Of 'Barbara of the House of Grebe' : '*That's* not a true story ; all the other *Noble Dames* are true stories'. Of *The Trumpet-Major* : 'That's one of the pretty ones'. Professor William Lyon Phelps of Yale University has more recently supplemented Miss Owen's record by informing us (in his *Autobiography*, p. 394) that Mrs. Hardy 'did not care much for Hardy's later novels'.

One day, when Rebekah Owen was passing Wareham House, next door to Max Gate, she saw several recently-excavated Roman skeletons lying in the garden. This sight aroused in her an intense desire to acquire some 'Roman remains' of her own ; and when she heard that a skull had been dug up in that part of Dorchester known as Fordington, she set about buying it. As soon as the skull was in her possession, she hurried to tell Hardy about it.

> Mr. Hardy was rather taken with the idea of my buying a Romano-British skull, and . . . said he must see it. Anent its name (given by me) Metellus, he recalled at once the conspirator and Cecilia Metella. I said . . . I fancied I should like to give Metellus a turn in the United States and then . . . he said : 'I should think he would much rather go to New York with you than to stay in Fordington. I am sure *I* should.' [3]

A few days later, Hardy departed for London. Mrs. Hardy did not go with him.

The winter of 1892–93 passed, and in the spring of 1893 the Henniker invitation to Dublin was renewed. This time there was no interference by 'crass casualty'. The Hardys went and spent several days with Lord Houghton and his sister. Shortly after Hardy's return to Max Gate, Mrs. Henniker also returned to England and, took up residence at Southsea, a section of Portsmouth which lies about seventy-five miles east of Max Gate. Letters began to flit back and forth between the two novelists. They exchanged books : in June, Hardy gave her a *Tess* ; in July, a copy of *A Laodicean* ; in September, a copy of *Desperate Remedies*. In October, they began to collaborate in writing a gruesome story called 'The Spectre of the Real'. This occasioned frequent meetings, often at Winchester, half-way between Southsea and Dorchester. When the weather was good, Hardy could bike thither. In his poem 'The Coming of the End' he refers to 'That journey of one day a week'. In 1894 Florence Henniker published a book of short stories entitled *Outlines*. It was dedicated 'To my friend Thomas Hardy'. She gave him a copy of the book in February 1894.

All of this activity with Mrs. Henniker naturally and inevitably had its effect on the atmosphere at Max Gate. In his letters written at this time to his wife, Hardy began addressing her as 'my dear Em' — not as 'My dearest Emmie' or 'Dearest Em' as he had previously done.[4] Instead of signing them 'Ever your affectionate husband', he now wrote 'Yours affectly'. Emma was later to scoff at the word. In the letter to be cited shortly she remarked : 'I scarcely think that love proper . . . is in the nature of men — as a rule — theirs being akin to children's, a sort of easy affectionateness'.

In a chapter on 'The First Mrs. Hardy', which I wrote twenty-five years ago, I remarked that 'in the poem "The Division" Hardy records his feeling that, though living under the same roof [with Emma],

> . . . I am here, and you are there,
>   And a hundred miles between ! . . .

> But that thwart thing betwixt us twain,
>   Which nothing cleaves or clears,
> Is more than distance, Dear, or rain,
>   And longer than the years !' [5]

In other words, I assumed that the 'you' of the poem was Emma Lavinia Hardy and that the 'hundred miles' between him and her were psychological or metaphorical miles, symbolizing the chasm now yawning between them. But in *Thomas Hardy: A Bibliographical Study*, Professor Richard Little Purdy recently stated : '"The Division" . . . is to be associated with Mrs. Henniker. . . . A draft of the poem . . . offering a different version of the last stanza . . . is now in my possession.' [6] We are not told what that 'different version' is, or what the nature of its evidence is, but it is clearly implied that the 'you' of the poem is Mrs. Henniker and that the 'hundred miles' are geographical (not metaphorical) miles — the distance, in round numbers, between Dorchester and Southsea. Professor Purdy also states (p. 344) that 'Mrs. Hardy's growing eccentricities were painfully manifest' during that May 1893 visit to Dublin.

What, then, is 'that thwart thing betwixt us twain' ? and between whom ? If 'you' does refer to Mrs. Henniker, the 'thwart thing' would presumably be the fact that both she and Hardy were married. But Hardy did not call her 'Dear', or even 'Florence'. His letters to her are addressed to 'My dear Mrs. Henniker', or (later) to 'My dear friend'. If, on the other hand, 'you' refers to Emma Hardy, 'that thwart thing' may be her disapproval of his growing interest in Mrs. Henniker. No matter how 'innocent' that interest may have been, Emma's eyes were sufficiently open to Hardy's emotional involvement to account for her 'growing eccentricities'. One has to remember, too, that Mrs. Henniker was not the first lady to take Hardy's eye or stir his emotions. Mrs. Hardy could easily have named others : Mary Jeune (later Lady St. Helier), for example. In any case, it is clear that Emma Hardy is closely concerned with the situation described in 'The Division', and the poem is accordingly included in this book,[7] even though some readers may still prefer to regard the verses as addressed to Florence Henniker.

Before leaving this poem, it should be stated that there is no reason for thinking that 'The Division' expresses Mrs. Henniker's own view of things. *Her* marriage was not on the rocks. By 1896 Lieutenant Henniker had become Major Henniker. Hardy called on him (and his wife) on 2 February 1896, and thought him 'really a very good fellow'. He eventually rose to be a Major-General, and when he died in 1912 Hardy wrote a little poem of three quatrains in his memory — a poem which Mrs. Henniker published in a book of obituary tributes to her husband. All of this leads one to the conclusion that, whatever awareness there was of a 'thwart thing' in 1893, it was an awareness in Hardy's mind, not in Florence Henniker's. That *he* was aware of a 'division' there can be no doubt, but it was from Emma that he felt divided. The poem 'Had You Wept' makes that fact quite clear. There he remarks :

. . . though you suffer as much as I from storms the hours
   are bringing
Upon your heart and mine, I never see you shed a tear. . . .

When I bade me not absolve you on that evening or the
   morrow,
Why did you not make war on me with those who weep
   like rain ?
You felt too much, so gained no balm for all your torrid
   sorrow,
And hence our deep division, and our dark undying pain.[8]

A sad poem, not a great one ; but a very revealing cry from the heart. In another poem of three poignant (if rather unpoetic) stanzas, 'Without, Not Within Her',

Hardy comments awkwardly on how 'out from his spirit flew death, and bale, and ban', from a soul 'whereon no thought of yours tarried two moments'.[9]

The situation in which Hardy now found himself brought him deep distress. His was, after all, a sensitive heart; and as the 1890's wore on, he came, more and more, to wish he had no heart at all.

> I look into my glass,
>   And view my wasting skin,
> And say, 'Would God it came to pass
>   My heart had shrunk as thin !'
>
> For then, I, undistrest
>   By hearts grown cold to me,
> Could lonely wait my endless rest
>   With equanimity.[10]

The disappointment of his fond hopes is given touching expression in 'Memory and I' — a poem that begins 'O Memory, where is now my youth?' The last six lines read :

> O Memory, where is now my love,
> That rayed me as a god above ?
>
> I saw her in an ageing shape
>   Where beauty used to be ;
> That her fond phantom lingers there
>   Is only known to me.[11]

One other painful poem must be included in this record of a distressing decade in Hardy's life. It is the most unpleasant example of back-biting in his poetic list. As a rule Hardy did not retaliate on his wife : he preferred to 'ache deep, but make no moans ; smile out, but stilly suffer'. But in 'You Were the Sort that Men Forget' he speaks out.[12] Here he does strike back. He speaks of Emma's lack of social 'art', of her 'words inept' that offended everybody, of her failure to understand 'friends whose mode was crude', and of her over-valuation of 'the courtesies of the bland'.

Of all the personal characteristics put on record in this poem by the sorrowing but critical husband, none received more frequent corroboration from other observers than Emma Hardy's addiction to 'words inept'. There were many such observers. Desmond MacCarthy remembered her saying to him sharply at tea one day : 'If you listen to what *I* am saying, you will find it as well worth hearing as Mr. Hardy's remarks'. Rebecca West once heard her say : 'Try to remember, Thomas Hardy, that you married a lady !' When a French writer, M. Henri Davray, called at Max Gate, he left with the impression that Hardy was 'timid and resigned to a situation he could not improve'. When the novelist set about writing *Jude the Obscure*, the 'words inept' multiplied. Dr. Fred B. Fisher (the Hardys' physician) came one day to call at Max Gate. Mrs. Hardy told him that she had made up her mind that 'she would never have anything more to do with any book her husband wrote'. She made it clear that she thought the new story he was now engaged in producing was just *too* vulgar for words. Mrs. Hardy was, of course, by no means alone in taking this view of *Jude the Obscure*. Jeannette L. Gilder was 'shocked and appalled by this story. . . . Aside from its immorality, there is its coarseness which is beyond belief' (*New York World*, 8 December 1895).

Mrs. Hardy, however, was not content with denouncing *Jude* to her doctor. She made a special trip up to London and

applied to Dr. Richard Garnett at the British Museum for aid in inducing her husband to burn his vicious manuscript.

She had already written Garnett to no avail ; now she implored him ; she wept. The young Garnetts, on hearing the story, were appalled or amused, depending upon their own individual leanings. But between gasps and snickers the news got around in the British Museum that Dr. Garnett had been appealed to, as Dean of Letters, for aid in suppressing this horrid book. In the end Mrs. Hardy returned, defeated, to Max Gate.[13]

Finished in March, *Jude the Obscure* was published on 1 November 1895. Three poems entitled 'In Tenebris' were written at this time of stress, when the world seemed to Hardy 'a welter of futile doing'. They are not included in the present volume because they are not addressed to Emma nor are they related, except indirectly, to her. But she stands there in the background ; she is still the Figure in the Scene.

In view of Mrs. Hardy's charge that her husband was 'very vain and very selfish' — T. P. O'Connor quotes her exact words — it is highly desirable that the testimony of other witnesses be placed alongside the wife's accusations. When Professor William Lyon Phelps of Yale University arrived, as a total stranger, at Max Gate in September 1900, he found Hardy 'looking rather frail and depressed. . . . Although he neither laughed nor smiled, he was, after the first moments, exceedingly gracious, kindly, and sympathetic.'[14] Phelps's comment is supported by that of other callers who found Hardy 'so modest, so unaware of his own great fame, so kind, natural, and unaffected, so free from jealousy and envy, that to listen to him, and to talk to him, was an inspiration'.[15] Nor did Hardy lose this freedom from vanity and this kindness as he grew older. In 1907 a New England poet who had been visiting in London wrote in her diary : 'Who turns out to be the most hospitable man of letters, the most prompt to reply to a note, and the most considerately mindful of me . . . ? Thomas Hardy !'[16]

Unfortunately, it was now impossible for Emma Hardy to see her famous husband in this light. The more the world paid attention to him, the more she seemed to resent it. Nor was it only society leaders like Lady Jeune, or novelists like Mrs. Henniker, or actresses like Mrs. 'Pat' Campbell, or admirers like Rebekah Owen, who curdled the milk of human kindness in Mrs. Hardy. There were others. Shortly after Hardy had finished writing *Jude the Obscure*, he had agreed to sit for his portrait. It was to be painted in oil by Miss Winifred Hope Thomson. She began work on the portrait in May 1895, but a month later she was forced by illness to call a halt. The sittings had taken place at 57 Onslow Square, London, where Miss Thomson lived with her sister Elspeth and their stepfather, a barrister named John Fletcher Moulton. In 1875 he had married Miss Thomson's mother, the widow of R. W. Thomson. The sittings for the portrait dragged on into 1896. In January of this year, Miss Thomson 'and Mr. Moulton' invited Hardy to come (obviously without Mrs. Hardy) and stay with them until the portrait had been completed. By this time Hardy knew Elspeth as well as her portrait-painting sister. Elspeth Thomson wrote poems. When she told Hardy that she often wrote them on the top of a bus, he replied that that was something *he* could not do — his attention on a bus top was 'always too distracted by the young women around me in fluffy blouses'. When Hardy wrote to Winifred Thomson to decline the invitation to stay at 57 Onslow Square, he sent his 'kind regards to your sister'. At this time Elspeth Thomson was thirty-seven years old. Three years after this, she married Kenneth Grahame, who was destined, a little later, to become world-famous as the author of *The Wind in the Willows*. Before Mrs. Grahame has been a month married, she had reason to wonder how a woman had best go about trying to insure the success of a marriage when her husband is a man of letters and a public figure. She thought of the Hardys, and so turned to Mrs. Hardy for advice. On 20 August 1899, Mrs. Hardy wrote her reply:

It is really too early days with you to be benefited by advice from one who has just come to the [end of her] twenty-fifth year of matrimony. . . . I can scarcely think that love proper, and enduring, is in the nature of men — as a rule — perhaps there is no woman 'whom custom will not stale.' There is ever a desire to give but little in return for our devotion, and affection. . . . Keeping separate a good deal is a wise plan in crises — and being both free — and expecting little, neither gratitude, nor attentions, love, nor *justice*, nor anything you may set your heart on — Love interest, — adoration, and all that kind of thing is usually a failure — complete — some one comes by and upsets your pail of milk in the end. . . . Years of devotion count for nothing — Influence can seldom be retained as years go by, and *hundreds* of wives go through a phase of disillusion — it is really a pity to have any ideals in the first place.[17]

It is unlikely that Hardy ever saw this unhappy letter, or knew its contents, but he did not need to. He was already aware of the fact that all genial warmth had disappeared from his life at Max Gate. As the nineteenth century straggled towards its drab end in December 1900, Hardy sat composing the lines of 'The Darkling Thrush'. All 'fervour' had gone out of him.

> The ancient pulse of germ and birth
> Was shrunken hard and dry,
> And every spirit upon earth
> Seemed fervourless as I.

VII

'DAGGERS OF DISTRESS'

WHEN the London *Graphic* printed Hardy's 'Darkling Thrush' on 29 December 1900, Mrs. Hardy promptly set about writing a poem of her own about a thrush. The poem has ten lines, but four of them will doubtless be enough to satisfy the reader's curiosity :

> There's a song of a bird in a tree, —
> A song that is fresh, gay, and free,
> The voice of a last summer's thrush,
> Shaking out his trills — hush ! hush !

If the reader is surprised to discover that Emma Lavinia Hardy could compose verses, it was (in 1900) no surprise to her husband. He had learned this fact when, earlier in this same year, she had given a public demonstration of her poetic abilities. A new magazine had made its appearance in London in January — the *Sphere*, edited by Clement K. Shorter — and to its very first number Hardy had contributed his poem 'At the War Office'. Three months later, the editor was startled to receive a poem from Mrs. Hardy. It was called 'Spring Song'. What was Clement Shorter to do with it ? He finally printed it (14 April 1900) with this wry comment : 'We all know that Mr. Thomas Hardy began his literary career by writing poems. It is interesting to know that his wife has also written poems. Mrs. Hardy sends me the following verses, which I am happy, as one of the most enthusiastic admirers of her husband's books, to print in the *Sphere*.'

A year later, Mrs. Hardy had another poetic inspiration. This time she wrote a poem called 'The Gardener's Ruse', giving a twenty-line account of the Dorset habit of planting an onion near the roots of a rose-bush —

> For the onion was bound to make roses sound,
> And a fine rich perfume to win.

She sent these verses to the editor of *The Academy*, and on 27 April 1901 he printed them with the editorial tongue-in-cheek comment that, 'This week Mrs. Thomas Hardy tells us in the following interesting lines how rose trees are planted in Wessex'.

One day, when Ford Madox Ford called at Max Gate and found Hardy out, Mrs. Hardy entertained him by reading what Ford called 'her own innocuous poems'. Some of them were about her cats. But she had other subjects of inspiration as well. Her husband had written (in *Tess*) about dancing maidens at Marlott. Emma Hardy entitled one of *her* poems 'Dancing Maidens'. The reader must be allowed to hear at least four lines from this poem:

> . . . the gay little maids they danced all day,
> Though in grief for their mother — that was their way.
> 'O, mother come back, come back, come back,'
> They cried as they danced all three, alack!

Many years before this, when Hardy had escorted Emma Gifford from Bath to the Wye Valley, they had paused at Tintern Abbey, and had there recited some of the famous lines about the place where Wordsworth had felt

> A presence that disturbs me with the joy
> Of elevated thoughts ; . . .
> . . . of setting suns,
> And the round ocean and the living air,
> And the blue sky. . . .

Now, Emma Hardy felt moved to give expression to her own 'elevated thoughts' about the blue sky. In 'A Blue-Day Orison' she exclaimed exultantly :

> With leaps and bounds the soul does run
> To greet this morn so lovely well begun,
> Filling the heart with high delight,
> To see so fair a morn so handsome bright.

There was, however, no exultation in the heart of her husband. In 'I Said to Love' (published in 1902) he wrote of 'features pitiless and iron daggers of distress'.[1] His distress was so great that even the once-loved music that Emma had played for him in the early days of his visits to St. Juliot no longer had power to move him. In 'Lost Love' he imagines Emma as saying to herself :

> I play my sweet old airs . . .
> But he does not balk
> His determined walk,
> And passes up the stairs.

> I sing my songs once more,
> And presently hear
> His footstep near
> As if it would stay ;
> But he goes his way,
> And shuts a distant door.[2]

The sound of the shutting of that distant door was to haunt Hardy's memory ten years later, when Emma was no longer there to play and sing her 'sweet old airs'.

Behind that shut door, Hardy did his best to forget, to lose himself in work, to let the composition of *The Dynasts* efface from his memory the 'sore smartings of the past'. During the daytime, while he was seated at his desk, he might persuade himself that, in his diligent analysis of Napoleon's military campaigns, he (Hardy) had forgotten his own scars.

But closely scanning in the night
I saw them standing crimson-bright
Just as she made them :
Nothing could fade them. . . .[3]

Hardy found relief from his pain, however, in an unexpected way, even though it meant that Emma's pail of milk was to be once again upset.

Some time in 1904 Mrs. Florence Henniker came to Max Gate to call, bringing with her a young friend, Miss Florence Emily Dugdale. The latter was then twenty-five years old. She, too, had literary ambitions, and eventually became known as the author of half a dozen or more children's books. None of them ever achieved the success of Beatrix Potter's famous stories, but Miss Dugdale's *Adventures of Mr. Prickleback* and her *Book of Baby Birds* at least escaped the undesirable fate of drawing forth wry editorial comments.

Miss Dugdale lived in London. Her residence there made it possible for her to offer to be of service to Hardy in connection with his further researches for *The Dynasts*, and it was not long before she was looking up various matters for him in the British Museum. She made it clear, too, that she took delight in thus being of service to him. He reciprocated by helping her with *her* work. When she wrote a story called 'Blue Jimmy, the Horse-Stealer' (it was eventually published in the *Cornhill*, February 1911), Hardy wrote out a number of lines for insertion into her text. As with Florence Henniker in 1893, so with Florence Dugdale in the years that followed her first call at Max Gate, Hardy took obvious delight in sharing the labours of literary composition with younger writers.

In later years Miss Dugdale was sometimes referred to as Hardy's secretary, but she herself denied — and did so in writing — that she had ever been his hired or paid secretary. She worked for him for the sheer pleasure of helping a famous author. He showed his gratitude for her help by giving her books. In June 1907 he inscribed a copy of *Wessex Poems* 'To Miss Florence Dugdale, with the Author's kind regards'.

On 22 June 1907 Hardy accompanied his wife to the Royal Garden Party at Windsor Castle. Among the other guests on this occasion were the French portrait-painter Jacques-Emile Blanche and his wife. Thanks to the fact that Monsieur and Madame Blanche travelled to Windsor with the Hardys, we know what happened, for Blanche never forgot the incident, and later wrote about it. Upon arriving at Windsor, the guests discovered that there were not enough conveyances at the station to transport them all up the steep hill to the Castle. Mrs. Hardy, who was wearing a long green veil, promptly took a seat in one of the royal carriages and invited Mme Blanche to come and sit beside her.

The latter declined, urging Hardy to take the seat and spare himself in the July-like heat. The author had just passed his sixty-seventh birthday and looked even older. Rheumatism had so lamed his back that on a previous occasion he had found it impossible to walk downstairs. He was obviously frail. Other guests headed for Windsor Castle followed Mme. Blanche's example in urging Hardy to ride. But Mrs. Hardy settled the matter. 'Mr. Hardy ride? That walk up the hill in the sun will do him a lot of good.' So up the stony hill Thomas Hardy and the portrait-painter trudged on foot, following the open carriage with its driver in King Edward's scarlet livery and its lady in a green veil, seated under a bright silk umbrella.[4]

Two years later, Hardy published a book of poems entitled *Time's Laughingstocks*. It contains one poem, 'The End of the Episode', in which, despite Hardy's urging himself to 'make no moans', we can hear the stoical echo of that visit to Windsor Castle :

> Ache deep ; but make no moans :
> Smile out ; but stilly suffer :
> The paths of love are rougher
> Than thoroughfares of stones.[5]

A month after the trip to Windsor (*i.e.* in July 1907), Hardy gave Florence Dugdale a copy of *The Rubáiyát*, inscribed simply 'F. E. D. from T. H.' — a book in which she could read (as thousands of other young ladies before and since have read) that, if only there were

> Thou
> Beside me singing in the Wilderness
> Oh, Wilderness were Paradise enow !

Miss Dugdale was no prophet ; she therefore had no way of foreseeing that a score of years later Hardy would be asking her to open that book and from it read to him as he lay on his death-bed.

A year later, Hardy inscribed a copy of the *Poems* of William Barnes to 'Miss F. E. Dugdale, with the Editor's kind regards'. In 1909 he gave her a copy of *The Mayor* ; later still, a copy of *Tess* inscribed 'To Florence Emily Dugdale, with best wishes from Thomas Hardy'.

During all this passage of time, Hardy was trying to take his own advice to 'ache deep . . . but stilly suffer'. As we have already noted, Henri Davray's opinion was that Hardy was 'timid'. Hardy himself preferred to call it 'tolerant', and he meant that word in its Latin sense : enduring, forbearing. In his poem 'Tolerance' he declared that

> at each cross I would surmise
> That if I had willed not in that wise
> I might have spared me many sighs.

> But now the only happiness
> In looking back that I possess . . .
>
> Is to remember I refrained
> And for my tolerance was disdained.[6]

In preparing to write the third part of *The Dynasts*, Hardy had learned about Lord Uxbridge, who, upon being hit by a cannon ball at Waterloo, exclaimed : 'I've lost my leg, by God !' Hardy had deliberately decided on a course of the same sort of uncomplaining fortitude — of grim endurance under painful experience. In 'The Wound' he refers to

> that wound of mine
> Of which none knew,
> For I'd given no sign
> That it pierced me through.[7]

Nothing gives better evidence of this determination to 'give no sign' than the 'tolerant' letters he wrote to Mrs. Hardy throughout these painful years.[8]

In 'When Oats Were Reaped' Hardy took pleasure in remembering — or at any rate in *thinking* — that Emma did 'not know that she wounded me !' When he wrote this poem, he could sorrowfully confess that 'I . . . now know well I wounded *her*',[9] but the agony of his own lacerated feelings had made previous recognition of his own mistakes and deficiencies impossible for him.

When the king appointed the author of *The Dynasts* to the Order of Merit, Hardy went to Marlborough House on 19 July 1910 to be invested. Mrs. Hardy did not accompany him. She was at Max Gate. Since we have none of the letters she wrote him, we must guard carefully against jumping to conclusions. Perhaps she did write to congratulate him on this honour. But I doubt it. The only reference Hardy himself made to the Order of Merit — that is, in the letters to his wife — is found in the letter in which he asked her to 'Put "O.M." *only*, on the envelope after my name'.[10]

Hardy was now seventy years old, weary, worn, and sad. The rosy colour of the Cornish romance of forty years ago had faded. And now

> There shall remain no trace
> Of what so closely tied us,
> And blank as ere love eyed us
> Will be our meeting-place.[11]

The fire on the hearth at Max Gate had gone out.

In one room at Max Gate, however, there was activity. There, through the year 1910 and into 1911, Emma Lavinia Hardy sat, writing her 'Recollections'. She described her birth and girlhood in Plymouth, her meeting with Hardy in 1870, and her marriage to him in 1874, and then filled the final pages of her manuscript (according to the testimony of the second Mrs. Hardy) with 'venom, hatred, and abuse of him and his family'.[12] Emma reached the last line of this autobiographical record and dated it : 'January 4, 1911'.

Having finished this unhappy task (and of course saying nothing about it to her husband), Mrs. Hardy next turned to collecting her poems. Before the year 1911 was over, she had the satisfaction of seeing in print a little book called *Alleys* (Dorchester : F. G. Longman, 1911). To that book the reader is indebted for whatever pleasure he may have received from her lines quoted in the present chapter of this introduction. There is, of course, no point in making any comment here on the obvious fact that these poems have attracted little attention in the past half-century.

VIII

'THE STRANGE HOUSE'

THOMAS HARDY's poems provide us with a curious kind of step-ladder on which we can mount and peer through the windows of Max Gate during the year 1912. The reader of these poems is likely to have an uncomfortable feeling of playing Paul Pry. In the *Life* of Ruskin we read about how Miss Rose LaTouche came one day and peered through the windows of Brantwood and saw the elderly John Ruskin seated there alone. In 1912 *we* come on many a day and peer through the windows of Max Gate, and see the elderly Emma Lavinia Hardy seated there alone. She is sometimes at her piano, sometimes at her desk, sometimes putting on her wraps in preparation for going out for a drive — but almost always alone.

We see her first at her desk. Having 'published' her collected poems, *Alleys*, she was now preparing a companion volume in prose. She called it *Spaces*, and described it as an 'Exposition of Great Truths'. She divided her book into four parts. Part 1 deals with 'The High Delights of Heaven', where there will be 'ease of locomotion — whether by wings or otherwise'. Part 2 is about 'Acceptors and Non-Acceptors', and describes 'the plan of Salvation prepared to rescue many . . . from Satan's power'. We know at least one 'Non-Acceptor' at Max Gate. Part 3 is about Hell. It gives a vivid description of 'the Last Day . . . when suddenly a spot of light will appear in the East at 4 o'clock a.m. according to western time — and dark night of Eastern time or about that hour . . . and . . . bodies will be seen rising and floating in the phosphorescent great oceans. . . .' Part 4 is entitled 'Retrospect'. When Mrs. Hardy's 'exposition' of these Great Truths was completed, F. G. Longman of Dorchester 'published' *Spaces* in a format similar to that of *Alleys*.

On another day when we see Emma at her desk, she is writing a letter to her absent husband. He is again in London, staying once more with Lady St. Helier, as he has been doing off and on throughout the past twenty-five years. What Emma said to him we do not know, for he eventually destroyed her letters to him, just as he destroyed the 'venomous' part of her *Recollections* when they finally came to his attention ; but we know how he *felt* one day, later on, when he happened upon that last letter :

> I chance now on the last of hers,
>   By the moon's cold shine ;
> It is the one remaining page
> Out of the many shallow and sage
>   Whereto she set her sign.
> Who could foresee there were to be
>   Such missives of pain and pine
> Ere I should read this last of hers
>   By the moon's cold shine ! [1]

On another occasion, when we peer through the windows of Max Gate, we see Emma seated at the piano with sheets and sheets of music stacked up in front of her. Hardy pauses a moment on his way out of the house, and she looks up from her playing long enough to speak to him :

> 'I am playing my oldest tunes,' declared she,
>   'All the old tunes I know, —
> Those I learnt ever so long ago.'

Instead of staying to listen, her husband walks out and is gone for two hours. When he comes back, Emma is still playing.

> When I returned from the town at nightfall
> > Notes continued to pour
> As when I had left two hours before:
> 'It's the very last time,' she said in closing;
> > 'From now I play no more.'[2]

And she didn't. It is easy to see why. Hardy's indifference now to her playing had destroyed for her all interest in the old songs. There had once been a time when the sound of the piano would catch his attention and keep him at home. But that time was past. They had now been married thirty-eight years. Mrs. Hardy had tried to rekindle the fire on the cold hearth by means of the old songs, but — as he later confessed with rueful honesty —

> I would not welcome it ;
> And for all I then declined
> O the regrettings infinite
> When the night-processions flit
> > Through the mind ![3]

His regrets were so sharp that, in after years, he came back, in poem after poem, to this subject of her peace-offering and his rejection of it. In 'An Upbraiding' he imagined her as speaking to him from the grave :

> Now I am dead you sing to me
> > The songs we used to know,
> But while I lived you had no wish
> > Or care for doing so.[4]

And, in the bitterness of his regrets, he refused to flinch but laid the lash on his own conscience, as he imagined her asking, pointedly : 'When *you* are dead . . . will you be cold, as when we lived, or how ?'[4]

In 'Penance' he describes how he now sits in the cold room, where there is 'not a spark within the grate', and stares at the silent piano with its 'chill old keys', and remembers his own defection. 'I would not join', he confesses ;

> I would not stay,
> But drew away,
> Though the winter fire beamed brightly.[5]

When it was all too late, he could

> look in her face and say,
> 'Sing as you used to sing . . .'
> But she hints not Yea or Nay . . .
> And dumb her lips remain.[6]

Sixteen years after her death, Hardy was still hearing Emma play her old songs, but sometimes he now found a previously unsuspected meaning in the words she sang.

> 'Now shall I sing
> That pretty thing
> "The Mocking-Bird" ?' — And sing it straight did she.

> But after years
> Of hopes and fears . . .
> I found I had heard
> The Mocking-bird
> In person singing there to me that day.[7]

In one of the most striking of his poems reminiscent of Emma's piano-playing, a poem in which he pictures Max Gate in the year A.D. 2000, he imagines another couple occupying his old home. Says one of them :

> 'I hear the piano playing —
>   Just as a ghost might play.'
> 'O — [replies the other] what are you saying ?
>   There's no piano to-day ;

Their old one was sold and broken ;
  Years past it went amiss.'
'—I heard it, or shouldn't have spoken :
  A strange house, this !' . . .

The house is old ; they've hinted
  It once held two love-thralls,
And they may have imprinted
  Their dreams on its walls.[8]

Those two love-thralls have indeed left their ghosts behind. 'They were queer in their works and ways.' Everybody said that Emma was 'queer'. But Hardy came to
recognize that he too had been 'queer' in *his* ways. He
makes his imaginary couple in the year 2000 scoff at
showing any interest whatsoever in those

Who loved, laughed, wept, or died here,
  Knew joy, or despair.[8]

But if we had no concern for the two who loved, laughed,
wept, and died at Max Gate, we would not be reading
or writing this book.

In 'The Walk' Hardy tells us why he often went
alone when he set out from Max Gate on a stroll. 'You
were weak and lame', he says with unchivalrous blunt-
ness :

So . . . I went alone, and I did not mind,
  Not thinking of you as left behind.[9]

But even when it was not a case of walking but of driving,
Mrs. Hardy often had to go alone. 'I drove not with
you', he sadly admits in 'Your Last Drive'. She had
gone off in an open car for a drive to Stinsford and five
miles beyond, and by the hour of her return the lights of
Dorchester were aglow in the late-November dusk. Upon
her arrival back at Max Gate, she was eager to talk about

the beauty of the scene — 'the charm of that haloed view'. But Hardy did not sit 'at her side that eve' and admitted that he 'missed her not'. The last two stanzas of 'Your Last Drive' take on additional poignancy when we realize all the conditions surrounding that final motor-trip. What bitter regret Hardy packed into the words he placed, in remorseful imagination, upon Emma's lips :

> Should you censure me I shall take no heed,
> And even your praises no more shall need.[10]

In *The Later Years of Thomas Hardy* there appears (on page 154) the simple three-worded statement that, on 25 November 1912, the day after Emma's seventy-second birthday, 'two ladies called'. The two were the Misses Rebekah and Catharine Owen, those 'good judges across the Atlantic'. After their departure, Mrs. Hardy went slowly upstairs. Hardy paid no attention to her going. He was out at the front gate, seeing the American ladies off. Forty hours later Mrs. Hardy was dead. Only later did he remember that on

> that calm eve when you walked up the stair,
> No thought soever
> That you might never
> Walk down again, struck me as I stood there.[11]

MRS. HARDY's death on 27 November 1912 was unexpected, but its effect on Thomas Hardy was even more
unexpected. That a heart as sensitive as his would feel
grief at the loss of his wife of thirty-eight years might
have been taken for granted ; that that grief would be
moderated by the relief he would likely feel as soon as
the irritations and barbs of recent years had finally ceased,
could be safely assumed by anyone familiar with his situation. That relief, however, might easily have been carried
over to the other side of the scales. Sir Walter Raleigh
once remarked that 'every fool knoweth that hatreds are
the cinders of affection'. In Hardy's case the cinders took
another form. There was no sign of hatred. Hardy
being Hardy, one might have guessed that. But no one
could have foreseen what actually happened. Once the
source of Hardy's unhappiness at Max Gate was removed
by the hand of death, his heart reacted by the production
of some of the tenderest poetry he had ever written.
Bitterness was forgotten. Love poem after love poem
surged up from the depths of his being, and before a
year had gone by, he had produced a body of verse which
is the chief reason for the present volume.

Some of the best of these tender and loving 'Poems
of 1912–13' were published in 1914 in a volume called
Satires of Circumstance, Lyrics and Reveries. Here they
stood as uncomfortable neighbours of the 'Satires of
Circumstance' which account for a part of the title of
the book. Hardy himself was aware of this incongruity.

When he and the second Mrs. Hardy were at work preparing the pages of *The Later Years of Thomas Hardy* (not to be published until after his death), he tried to pass these poems off as 'humorous productions which had been issued with a light heart before the war' (*Later Years*, p. 164). The twelve 'Satires' had appeared in the *Fortnightly Review* in April 1911, shortly after Mrs. Emma Hardy had finished writing her embittered *Recollections*. To call these satires 'humorous productions' is of course nonsense. And to pretend that they had been issued with a light heart is sillier still. Hardy's posthumous attempt to masquerade as a pre-war jester fooled no one. Even at the time of their first publication they were recognized as the most cynical and mordant comments Hardy had ever made on marriage and mismating. Edmund Gosse noticed the hard and bitter spirit in which these poems were written, and remarked : 'The wells of human hope have been poisoned for him by some condition of which we know nothing'. Gosse knew more than he was willing to admit in public. Hardy, in replying to Gosse's review of the 1914 volume, was equally evasive. 'The little group of satires cost me much sadness in having to reprint them in the volume.' This statement is partly true and partly false. No one need question the sadness : it was doubtless there. But Hardy did not *have* to reprint the satires of 1911 in the 1914 book. He did in fact omit one of them. He *could* have omitted all twelve ! But there can be no doubt about the truthfulness of the rest of Hardy's statement to Gosse about the little group of satires : 'The scales had not fallen from my eyes when I wrote them, and when I reprinted them they had'.

Once the scales had fallen from his eyes, Hardy saw things with clearer vision, even though his eyes were often filled with tears. The first of the 'Poems of 1912–13', entitled 'The Going', describes the effect upon him of Emma's sudden death, after 'giving no hint that night that . . . she would . . . up and be gone . . . never to bid good-bye . . . !'

> O you could not know
> That such swift fleeing—
> No soul foreseeing
> Not even I — would undo me so ! [1]

In 'Without Ceremony' Hardy muses on the fact that the suddenness of her death was so characteristic of the living woman. She had always acted in that impulsive way. She seemed to like 'to vanish without a word'. Hardy remembered how, on the evening when the two New York ladies called, he had gone out to the front portal of the Max Gate grounds and had watched Rebekah Owen's chauffeur light the gas lamps of the motor-car. By the time he re-entered the house, Emma had vanished upstairs.

> So, now that you disappear
>   For ever in that swift style,
> Your meaning seems to me
> Just as it used to be :
>   'Good-bye is not worth while !' [2]

He had always been a man for remembering dates and anniversaries, and now he had a new one to add to his list — the date of her death in 'that sad November' [3] — when she

> . . . lay by the window whence she had gazed
> So many times when blamed or praised,
> Morning or noon, through years and years,
> Accepting the gifts that Fortune bore,
> Sharing, enduring, joys, hopes, fears ! [3]

Her body lay there 'by the window' for two days before the funeral. Her shrouded presence left its mark upon his memory, and a year later he could still see

> Her who, before last year ebbed out,
> Was costumed in a shroud.[4]

Her now-silent lips reminded him of the day when, at St. Juliot, he had kissed them for the first time. Later he had
> kissed them in love, in troth, in laughter,
> When she knew all ; long so !
> That I should kiss them in a shroud thereafter
> She did not know.[5]

In another poem Hardy tried to recall the last time he had kissed his wife. 'But . . . I read no *finis* in it, as at [the] closing of a book.' Later, however, he remembered that it *was* the last time —

> When, at a time anon,
> A figure lay stretched out whitely,
> And I stood looking thereon.[6]

When the day of the funeral came — Saturday, 30 November — Hardy

> . . . watched the rain-smitten back of the car
> When it started forth for a journey afar
> Into the sullen November air.
>
> I have seen many gayer vehicles. . . .
> But I don't forget that rain-smitten car,
> Knowing what it bore ![7]

After reading 'Days to Recollect' and other poems of reminiscence like it, the reader may have acquired the impression that Hardy's resurgence of love for the departed Emma was the result of the passage of time.

'Time is the only comforter', Jane Welsh once remarked to Thomas Carlyle. In Hardy's case, however, it was not a matter of the passing of time. The resurgence of love was immediate. That is one of the surprising aspects of this Cornish romance. Before Emma's body had been lowered into the grave in the Stinsford churchyard, Hardy had not only revived within himself the long-cooled affection for his wife, but had also decided on a public announcement of that revival. The significance of his act was not lost on those who attended Mrs. Hardy's funeral on 30 November. Let Miss Rebekah Owen, who was present, be the one to describe the occasion :

> I was greatly touched by the scene, the lonely churchyard, the pale November sunlight, the very few who were there — Mr. Hardy, his brother and sisters, a deputation from some Dorchester society, a very few villagers, the Leslies [the Reverend Edward C. Leslie and his wife] and ourselves. She who was in many respects Elfride [of the Blue Eyes] was laid to rest near the great vault described in *A Pair of Blue Eyes*. To those who knew her as well as we did the sad inscription on Mr. Hardy's wreath had double pathos — 'From her lonely husband — with the old affection'. I think it was meant for all who had known her, — the one outspoken word of a silent man.[8]

From that date on, the grave in the Stinsford churchyard became one of the shrines in Hardy's list of holy places. Pilgrimages were regularly made to it. The grass was kept cut ; flowers were often carried to the grave. Florence Dugdale was called upon to make so many such visits with the bereaved poet that one day, in a letter to Rebekah Owen, she burst out with an irritated reference to 'the "late espousèd saint"'.[9] Hardy's thoughts often turned to that grave. Two months after the funeral, when it was still mid-winter, he was already looking forward to the spring when

> Soon will be growing
>   Green blades from her mound,
> And daisies be showing
>   Like stars on the ground,
> Till she form part of them —
> Ay — the sweet heart of them,
> Loved beyond measure
> With a child's pleasure
> All her life's round.[10]

For Hardy, Emma's grave had no forbidding aspect. *She* wasn't there; *that* he knew. Her spirit would have flitted off promptly to Cornwall; of that, one could be sure. He imagined her saying to him:

> My spirit will not haunt the mound
>   Above my breast,
> But travel, memory-possessed,
> To where my tremulous being found
>   Life largest, best. . . .
>
> And there you'll find me. . . .[11]

And in his thoughts that is where he did find her, just as he had done back in 1870.

> I found her out there
> On a slope few see,
> That falls westwardly
> To the salt-edged air . . .
>
> I brought here here,
> And have laid her to rest
> In a noiseless nest
> No sea beats near.[12]

As he mused on the contrast between St. Juliot and Stinsford, an amusing thought struck him. When Emma was living in Cornwall, she always gazed westward. No matter what the weather,

> Wind foul or fair,
> Always stood she
> Prospect-impressed ; . . .
> Never elsewhere
> Seemed charm to be.

And now, by one of 'life's little ironies',

> Always eyes east
> Ponders she now — . . .
> Never the least
> Room for emotion
> Drawn from the ocean
> Does she allow.[13]

By another irony of fate, Emma Hardy's remains were now lying near the grave of Louisa Harding, the farmer's daughter who had captured Hardy's eye and fancy in his boyhood. *The Early Life* tells us (p. 33) that he had once mustered up enough courage to murmur 'Good evening' to her, as he passed her in the lane at Higher Bockhampton. Louisa made no reply, and that 'Good evening' was the only word Hardy ever said to her. She died some years later and was buried in the Stinsford churchyard. Emma had never known Louisa Harding, but now they were neighbours. Emma's grave sent Hardy's thoughts back to 'Louie the buoyant'. He remembered her 'gauzy muslin' and recalled her 'life-lit brow'. And now Emma, the Cathedral canon's niece, had joined the farmer's daughter : 'Long two strangers they and far apart ; such neighbours now !' [14]

The sheer quantity of the verses in which Emma Hardy's grave figures makes it impossible to linger long here on any one of the poems. In 'The Dream is —

Which ?' Hardy wanders 'through a mounded green / To find her, I knew where'.[15] In 'Lament'

> she is shut
> From friendship's spell
> In the jailing shell
> Of her tiny cell.[16]

In 'The Curtains Now Are Drawn' he 'stands there in the rain, with its smite upon her stone'.[17] In 'Something Tapped' he imagines her spirit saying to him :

> So cold it is in my lonely bed,
> And I thought you would join me soon.[18]

This voice from the grave continued to speak to Hardy with increasingly poignant insistence, and in a poem which deals specifically with 'the woman calling' to him, he achieves one of his greatest poetic successes. From the first line of 'The Voice' to the intense and heart-broken pathos of its close, this poem exhibits a perfect fusion of subject, mood, and technique. One can apply to it the words Alfred Noyes once used in commenting on another poem by Thomas Hardy : 'it bears upon it the stamp of a truth and sincerity beyond praise'.

> Woman much missed, how you call to me, call to me,
> Saying that now you are not as you were
> When you had changed from the one who was all to me,
> But as at first, when our day was fair.
>
> Can it be you that I hear ? Let me view you, then. . . .
>
> Thus I ; faltering forward,
> Leaves around me falling,
> Wind oozing thin through the thorn from norward,
> And the woman calling.[19]

Hardy dated this poem 'December 1912' — *i.e.* within a month of Mrs. Hardy's death. He had previously written in his notebook the observation that 'poetry is emotion put into measure. The emotion must come by nature, but the measure can be acquired by art' (*Later Years*, p. 78). He never showed more complete mastery of the art of poetic composition than when he wrote 'The Voice'.

In another poem he imagined Emma's voice speaking to him *before* her death :

> It will be much better when
> I am under the bough ;
> I shall be more myself, Dear, then,
> Than I am now. . . .
>
> And when you come to me
> To show you true,
> Doubt not I shall infallibly
> Be waiting you.[20]

The simplicity of the words, the seeming-spontaneity of the rhymes, ought not to conceal from the reader the technical perfection of this poem.

In 'The Prospect', written when December had succeeded the November of the funeral, Hardy describes the icy airs that 'wheeze through the skeletoned hedge from the north', and he feels 'a numbing that threatens snow'. He knows that boys will want to go sledging or ice-skating.

> But well, well do I know
> Whither I would go ![21]

And when he reaches the end of the year 1912, the thought most prominent in his mind is the fact that 'You are not here . . .' to wish him a Happy New Year.

> So it comes that we stand lonely
> In the star-lit avenue,
> Dropping broken lipwords only,
> For we hear no songs from you.[22]

Shakespeare's Ophelia once remarked : 'I would give you some violets, but they withered all when my father died'. Hardy's wreath in the Stinsford churchyard had doubtless 'withered all' before the end of the year 1912 ; but Emma's spirit had, by that date, no need of the wreath or of the words of its inscription ; for there were, by now, many words of greater permanence addressed to her 'from her lonely husband — with the old affection'.

'VETERIS VESTIGIA FLAMMAE'

IN Hardy's 1902 volume, *Poems of the Past and the Present*, there is a section of ten poems which were the result of his trip to Italy. He called this group 'Poems of Pilgrimage'. If he had not already made use of this heading in 1902, it would have served him well for use in some later volume, for almost as soon as Emma was buried, the poet began making sentimental pilgrimages to spots associated with her, and began writing poems about these pilgrimages. In 'Old Excursions' he explains why he enjoyed going to places 'as we used to do'. Simply because 'while walking weary, near me seemed her shade'.[1] St. Juliot, Tintagel, Beeny Cliff, Bossiney, Camelford, Pentargon Bay, Boscastle, Launceston, all were revisited. Even Plymouth, where Emma was born, was put on the list — Plymouth, the marble-streeted town to which he had promised to take her, but had never done so. Every shrine revisited had a poem written in its honour. As Sir Arthur Quiller-Couch shortly thereafter observed, all who knew Hardy in his later years became reverently aware that he had constructed 'a pure fairy-tale' of his Cornish romance and had bathed it in glowing colours, and that it took only a sight of a familiar scene to set the poet off retracing, reclothing, reliving the happy events of his dream.

Naturally enough, St. Juliot ranked first on the list of spots to be revisited, for 'much of my life claims the spot as its key',[2] and the day when Hardy had first gone there was a day never to be forgotten : 7 March 1870.

'This great date' he called it in his poem. 'Don't you know it? This day of the year, what rainbow-rays embow it!' [3] And forty-three years after that 'great date' he was back in Cornwall again.

This return to Lyonnesse was done with mixed feelings, for upon finding himself back at the scene where his Cornish romance had begun, conflicting emotions made themselves known. First, there were the Joys of Memory, of being able to

> begin again, as if it were new,
> A day of like date I once lived through,[4]

and under the inspiration of this joy a number of the poems we have already noticed were written. See, for example, 'St. Launce's Revisited', 'At Castle Boterel', 'Where the Picnic Was', and 'Beeny Cliff'. But Hardy's joy in seeing these places was marred by two thoughts from which he found it impossible to escape: one, that he was alone, whereas

> The woman now is — elsewhere — whom the ambling
> pony bore,
> And nor knows nor cares for Beeny, and will laugh there
> nevermore.[5]

and the other, that in the forty-year interval between his first visit and the present return, there had been much pain and sorrow for both of them:

> Summer gave us sweets, but autumn wrought division,[6]

and Hardy could not rid his mind of the memory of the long, cold winter of distress that had followed the autumnal 'division'. This thought preyed upon his mind all the more because he was, as G. M. Young has pointed out, 'a poet of reflection . . . his verses are, to a greater degree than is perhaps common with poets, a commentary — an

78

old man's commentary on a life that had not been happy'.[7]
He was haunted by the thought that he was partly responsible for the unhappiness. He had *not* always sought
Emma's company. Her imagined voice now came to
rebuke him :

> When I could let him know
> How I would like to join in his journeys
> Seldom he wished to go,
> But now he goes and wants me with him
> More than he used to do.[8]

On 6 July 1908 Hardy had written to his wife : 'I would
rather take you to Cornwall than about London'.[9] But
he had never acted on that offer. Now, when it is too
late, he sadly recalls that

> never I squired my Wessex girl
> In jaunts to Hoe or street
> When hearts were high in beat,
> Nor saw her in the marbled ways
> Where market-people meet
> That in her bounding early days
> Were friendly with her feet.[10]

No wonder he now has the feeling that a

> phantom draws me by the hand
> To the place — Plymouth Hoe —
> Where side by side in life, as planned,
> We never were to go ! [10]

Two other poems deal with his thoughts about Plymouth :
'Places', in which he thinks of Emma as lying in her
babyhood 'in a room by the Hoe, like the bud of a
flower' ; [11] and 'The Marble-Streeted Town', in which
he regrets that 'none here knows her history' and none
'has heard her name', even though there was a time when
she was 'the brightest of its native souls'.[12]

In 'The Clock of the Years' Hardy amuses himself with the idea of 'making the clock . . . go backward', and thus recapturing his lost wife. He watches Time turn backwards till Emma is as 'I first had known her'; but once started on its backward course, there was no stopping the clock at 1870. Soon 'she waned . . . to babyhood' at Plymouth, and then to 'nought at all'. Better, Hardy's conclusion is, 'Better she were dead'; for, even when dead and buried, the memory of her as alive could live on in him.[13]

Upon his return from his pilgrimage to Cornwall and Devon, Hardy set about making some needed renovations at Max Gate. Some of the rooms were repainted, some pictures were replaced, some new cups and saucers were acquired, and 'a formal-fashioned border' of flowers was constructed in the garden 'where the daisies used to be'. Emma had been very fond of daisies. The removal of her flowers made Hardy imagine that Emma's ghost would not approve of the changes he was making, and in 'His Visitor' he records her imagined words to him:

> I don't want to linger in this re-decked dwelling;
> I feel too uneasy at the contrasts I behold.[14]

And when, just a year after Mrs. Hardy's death, the garden at Max Gate was receiving the roots of two François Guillot rose bushes (the gift of Rebekah Owen) the same 'visitor' from the churchyard at Stinsford returned to make further imaginary comment on the Max Gate renovations:

> He built for me that manor-hall,
> And planted many trees withal,
> But no rose anywhere.
> And as he planted never a rose
> That bears the flower of love,
> Though other flowers throve,

> Some heart-bane moved our souls to sever
> Since he had planted never a rose ;
> And misconceits raised horrid shows,
> And agonies came thereof.[15]

The changes produced by the year 1913 were not confined to the house and grounds of Max Gate. Hardy was aware of changes in himself as well. In 'Paths of Former Time' he notes the fact that he

> can no more go
> By the summer paths we used to know ! [16]

In 'This Summer and Last' he addresses the 'unhappy Summer' of 1913 and declares that 'never, never will it be . . . to me' what the previous summer had been, when the rays of the summer sun had 'crept into corn-brown curls'.[17] Those curls had been brought back into his thoughts by his recent coming upon a locket in which he had kept the curl which Emma Lavinia Gifford had given him in 1870. Two poems grew out of that discovery : 'A Forgotten Miniature', in which Hardy spoke of Emma's 'beauties' as 'glowing as at first',[18] and 'On a Discovered Curl of Hair', in which the 'corn-coloured' hair is described as 'brightest brown'.[19] When the locket containing this 'curl of hair' was exhibited in April 1940 at the Grolier Club in New York City, the hair was described as 'darkened somewhat'.[20]

Going on pilgrimages, planning renovations, making discoveries, composing poems, planting rose bushes — none of these activities interfered with the accurate and punctual working of Hardy's memory. When November 1913 arrived, one might almost have prophesied that 'A Death-Day Recalled' would be written, in which the 'listless' poet would relive 'the hour of her spirit's speeding'.[21] In 'A Night in November', he describes how some dead leaves blew into his room and alighted upon his bed.

> One leaf of them touched my hand,
> And I thought that it was you
> There stood as you used to stand,
> And saying at last you knew ! [22]

One would like to think that, at last, Emma Hardy did 'know'. If *she* did not, at least the world knows — that is, that part of the world that reads English poetry — that Hardy had returned to the company of his first wife and had brought with him all 'the old affection'.

When, in November 1913, Hardy went to Cambridge to be invested in his honorary fellowship at Magdalene College, he told the President of the College, A. C. Benson, that he had been writing some poems about his wife but didn't know whether he ought to publish them or not. They were, he explained, 'very intimate, of course, but the verses came ; it was quite natural ; a loss like that makes one's old brain vocal !'

Hardy decided to publish. To one with the poet's memory for dates, it was title enough to call this group simply 'Poems of 1912–13'. But for the benefit of any reader who did not know the history of 1912 and 1913, Hardy added, as a sub-title, three words that he remembered, characteristically enough, from his studies of more than sixty years in the past. When he was still a schoolboy, his mother had given him a copy of Dryden's translation of Virgil's *Aeneid*. Shortly after this, Hardy began the study of Latin ; and by the time he embarked upon his work as an architect's apprentice under John Hicks, he was able to read Virgil in the original. By getting up at five o'clock in the morning, or (in the summer-time) even as early as four a.m., he was able to get through several books of the *Aeneid*. In this way he learned about

Dido and her pathetic love story. Her phrase about recognizing 'the traces of an old fire' — *veteris vestigia flammae* — had remained in Hardy's retentive memory for half a century, and when he was preparing to publish his own poetic 'vestiges' — the marks of his own flame of long ago — he decided to append Virgil's phrase as a secondary title for the 'Poems of 1912–13'.

The world has been unanimous in applauding the poet's decision to publish and thus admit outsiders into this 'very intimate' scrutiny of his Cornish romance. Edmund Blunden has called these poems 'the most unconventional and impressive elegies in English', and has declared that among them are 'some of a tender and lingering luxuriance'. Arthur McDowall observed that 'no modern poems of the kind are more wistfully tender than these ; they have a selfless pathos which transcends regret'. In commenting on these poems in 1940 (in his centennial biography of Hardy), the present editor remarked :

> It is entirely possible that the Poems of 1912–13 will outlive anything else that Hardy has done. . . . The title 'Poems of 1912–13' is convenient but colourless. They ought to be known by their secondary and more moving title : 'Veteris Vestigia Flammae'. The poet's bereavement is here recorded with a beauty, a tenderness, and a wistful restraint that attain an effect unique in English literature. No lover of poetry can read these verses without feeling tempted to regard the discord at Max Gate as well worth while. With Amiens in *As You Like It* one might say :
>
> > Happy is your Grace
> > That can translate the stubbornness of Fortune
> > Into so quiet and so sweet a style.[23]

Samuel C. Chew called these poems 'both touching and extraordinary, quite unlike any other elegies in the language'. In them, declared J. E. Barton, 'the thrill of grief is raised to monumental beauty'. When Professor C. Day Lewis addressed the Congress of the West Country Writers' Association at their meeting in Weymouth in June 1954, he remarked : 'Hardy's qualities of patience, moral courage and integrity are manifest in his poems. After his first wife's death, when he was seventy-two, he released some of the finest love poetry — the best in our language. No other English poet was so tender.' And Douglas Brown has, more recently, pointed to these verses as 'Hardy's supreme achievement in poetry ; among these elegies are his finest single poems'.

The last fifteen years of Hardy's life were spent in the pleasant glow of the rekindled embers. In this Indian Summer, every sight, every sound, served to recall his departed wife to his mind. 'A woman was playing.' So he writes in 'At the Piano'. The mere sight of her 'sent him mentally straying'.[24] Even the absence of sounds from the piano reminded him of Emma. At the door of Max Gate he pauses long enough to think 'no song-notes within the door now call to me'.[25] He sees a woman driving : the sight serves to remind him of what an expert horse-woman Emma had been. 'Where drives she now ? It may be where no mortal horses are.'[26] Even a shadow recalls her to his mind. He sees a shadow in the garden at Max Gate. It looks so much like

the shadow a well-known head and shoulders
Threw there when she was gardening

that he can hardly refrain from turning to speak to her ; but he resists the impulse to look, 'lest my dream should fade'.[27]

In the late summer of 1916, in spite of the difficulties which the war placed upon travel, Hardy made another trip to Cornwall — this time to see whether the marble tablet which he had designed in Emma's memory had been properly hung in St. Juliot Church. 'There it stands', he wrote on 8 September, '. . . the still marble, date-graven'.[28] But as he looked at it, he thought and regretted that no marble could record 'her glance, glide, or smile, nor . . . her voice. . . .'[28] In 'The Monument-Maker', he imagines his wife's 'sweet ghost' making — not sweet, but scornful — comments on the tablet he has just erected. 'You, who carve there your devotion . . . you felt none, my dear !' And when the ghost vanishes with those accusing words, Hardy ruefully concludes that he had 'never been truly known by her, and never prized !'[29]

Whether the ghost was scornful or appreciative, one thing was certain : the church at St. Juliot was the appropriate place for the erection of a memorial to Emma Lavinia Gifford. For there, as Hardy pointed out,

> she flourished sorrow-free,
> And, save for others, knew no gloom.[30]

His memory of the 'sorrow-free' girl with the flapping curls carried his thoughts back nearly half a century, and he was keenly aware of the fact that the tablet he had erected was *not* a memorial to an 'earthless essence'[31] but to a woman of flesh and blood. As he thought of 'the fond and fragile creature' he had first known at St. Juliot, he decided that he preferred her 'mortal mould', even though he had had recent and sorrowful experience with what the word mortality meant.[31]

Four years later Hardy made another pilgrimage, this time to a not-so-distant shrine. He was now eighty. On 22 August 1920, 'fifty years . . . to an hour' after he had gone with Emma to Beeny Cliff on that rainy day in 1870, he went to Stinsford to 'lay roses . . . on her monument . . . upon the luxuriant green'.[32] 'What might have moved you,' he asks himself in the poem, 'if you had known ?'[32]

Now that old age had made travel more difficult for him, Hardy was content to sit before the fire and let his imagination do the travelling for him. In a poem called 'The Seven Times' he reviews all his numerous trips to St. Juliot, identifying six moods in which he went to Lyonnesse 'and found her there'. Now that he is

> shrunken with old age and battering wear,
> An eighty-years long plodder,

he comes again — 'long after' that first meeting with the 'eyesome maiden' — but now

> catches no customed signal, hears no voice call,
> Nor finds her there.[33]

On 27 November 1922 Hardy again went to Stinsford. It was just ten years since Emma's death. He carried flowers and tidied up her grave, and in 'Ten Years Since' recorded other marks of the passage of time. The trees at Max Gate had grown ten feet taller,

> And the piano wires are rustier,
> The smell of bindings mustier
>   Than when, with casual look
>   And ear, light note I took
>   Of what shut like a book
>   Those ten years since ![34]

On 7 March 1924 Hardy entered in his notebook (just as if he needed any such reminder !) : 'E. first met 54 years ago'.

20 November 1925 saw the publication of the last of Hardy's books to be published during his lifetime : *Human Shows, Far Phantasies, Songs, and Trifles*. One of

the 152 poems in this book was entitled 'She Opened the Door'. At the end of the poem Hardy placed the date '1913', suggesting in this way that it might have been published earlier as one of the 'Poems of 1912–13' but that he had held this poem over in order to give it twelve years of polishing. It is a perfect summary of his Cornish romance. No better description of what Emma Lavinia Gifford had meant to him can be given :

> She opened the door of the West to me,
>   With its loud sea-lashings,
>   And cliff-side clashings
> Of waters rife with revelry.
>
> She opened the door of Romance to me,
>   The door from a cell
>   I had known too well,
> Too long, till then, and was fain to flee.
>
> She opened the door of a Love to me,
>   That passed the wry
>   World-welters by
> As far as the arching blue the lea.
>
> She opens the door of the Past to me,
>   Its magic lights,
>   Its heavenly heights,
> When forward little is to see ! [35]

A little over two years later, Emma opened one more door for him — the door of her tomb. Hardy died on 11 January 1928. Her grave in the Stinsford churchyard now carries a stone on which these words appear : 'Here lies the heart of Thomas Hardy'. That is doubly true. On one side of the tombstone are three words which Hardy himself had had carved there in 1912 : THIS FOR REMEMBRANCE. His poems help *us* to remember.

NOTES AND REFERENCES

In the notes that follow, the titles of Hardy's various books of poetry are abbreviated thus :

    CP—*Collected Poems* (1931)
    HS—*Human Shows, Far Phantasies* (1925)
    LL—*Late Lyrics and Earlier* (1922)
    MV—*Moments of Vision* (1917)
    PP—*Poems of the Past and the Present* (1902)
    SC—*Satires of Circumstance, Lyrics and Reveries* (1914)
    SP—*Selected Poems* (1916)
    TL—*Time's Laughingstocks* (1909)
    WP—*Wessex Poems* (1898)
    WW—*Winter Words* (1928)

The first page-reference after the title of an individual poem refers to the page in the present volume. The references that follow indicate (*a*) the first book-publication by Hardy, (*b*) any subsequent reprinting by him, and (*c*) the inclusion of the poem in *Collected Poems*. For example, in Chapter II of the introduction, note 9 reads : '"Beeny Cliff", p. 117. SC (119), SP (69), CP (330)'. This means that the text of the poem 'Beeny Cliff' is given on page 117 of this book ; that the poem was first published in *Satires of Circumstance* (page 119) ; that it was reprinted on page 69 of *Selected Poems*, and was finally gathered into *Collected Poems*, page 330. Only two of these love poems ('At the Word "Farewell"' and 'The Wound') made their *first* appearance in *Selected Poems* in 1916.

Eight of the poems which originally appeared in *MV* were subjected to textual revision before being published in *CP*; but only one poem in *LL* was thus revised, and no changes whatever were made in the poems first published in *HS*. Most of the revisions were of so slight a nature as to justify our ignoring them here. The text here followed is that of *CP*.

I. Journey into Lyonnesse

1. 'An Indiscretion in the Life of an Heiress', *New Quarterly Magazine*, July 1878.
2. *Under the Greenwood Tree* (Part I, Chapter 1), 1872.

3. Barrie, in a speech at the Society of Authors dinner, reported in the London *Morning Post*, January 1929.

4. The MS. of this sonnet (now in the Birmingham City Museum) entitles it 'Chance'. When Hardy published the sonnet in *WP* (1898, p. 7) he changed the title to 'Hap'.

5. *The Mayor of Casterbridge*, Chapter 32.

6. *Hardy and the Lady from Madison Square* (1952), p. 66.

7. *The Mayor of Casterbridge*, Chapter 11.

8. *The Mayor of Casterbridge*, Chapter 1.

9. *A Pair of Blue Eyes*, Chapter 2.

10. 'When I Set Out for Lyonnesse', p. 105. *SC* (20), *SP* (17), *CP* (293).

II. 'A WEEK'

1. 'The Wind's Prophecy', p. 106. *MV* (135), *CP* (464).

2. 'A Man Was Drawing Near to Me', p. 108. *LL* (38), *CP* (549).

3. 'The Discovery', p. 109. *SC* (80), *CP* (313).

4. 'St. Launce's Revisited', p. 110. *SC* (90), *CP* (335).

5. 'Green Slates', p. 111. *HS* (26), *CP* (675).

6. 'At Castle Boterel', p. 112. *SC* (121), *SP* (71), *CP* (330). Arthur McDowall remarks : 'A re-living and actuality of passion . . . rings in the mere rhythm of "At Castle Boterel" with an assurance uncommon in Hardy's verse' ; and J. E. Barton thinks that in this poem Hardy's 'qualitative sense of life is suggested with extraordinary power' and declares that this poem condenses 'so much of his atmosphere, passion and cadence that it may almost seem to epitomize him'.

7. 'A Dream or No', p. 114. *SC* (113), *SP* (65), *CP* (327). The emphatically anapestic rhythm of this poem,

> Yes, I have had dreams of that place in the West,
> And of how, coastward bound on a night long ago,

recalls the fact that this poem was written shortly after the death of Swinburne — an event which produced Hardy's poem 'A Singer Asleep'. Swinburne's addiction to anapests had made a marked impression on the younger poet. The reader who has not previously noted this fact may find it helpful to listen to Hardy's own testimony as recorded in a letter he once wrote to Swinburne :

> One day, when examining several English imitations of a well-known fragment of Sappho, I interested myself in trying to strike

out a better equivalent for it than the commonplace 'Thou, too, shalt die', etc., which all the translators had used during the last hundred years. I then stumbled upon your 'Thee, too, the years shall cover', and all my spirit for poetic pains died out of me.

Swinburne's anapests merely strengthened in Hardy another influence dating from his youthful violin-playing. In drawing up an account of himself for the 1916 edition of *Who's Who*, Hardy mentioned 'dance music' as one of his recreations.

8. 'A Duettist to her Pianoforte', p. 115. *LL* (51), *CP* (555).

9. 'Beeny Cliff', p. 117. *SC* (119), *SP* (69), *CP* (330). Early in September 1938 Siegfried Sassoon went to St. Juliot, which he called 'the scene of long lost romance'. A month later he wrote Sir Sydney Cockerell : 'When I got home, I re-read the 1912–13 poems ; how queer and unique they are. I'd always admired 'Beeny Cliff' tremendously but the others now seemed equally fascinating in their less lyrical way.'

10. 'The Phantom Horsewoman', p. 118. *SC* (125), *SP* (73), *CP* (332).

11. 'Places', p. 120. *SC* (123), *CP* (331).

12. 'The Old Gown', p. 121. *LL* (48), *CP* (554).

13. 'The Frozen Greenhouse', p. 122. *HS* (78), *CP* (698).

14. 'At the Word "Farewell"', p. 123. *SP* (18), *MV* (11), *CP* (405). Referring to these verses, Hardy once remarked to Vere H. Collins : 'This is quite a good poem'.

15. 'As 'Twere To-Night', p. 124. *LL* (42), *CP* (551).

16. 'A Week', p. 125. *SC* (165), *CP* (356).

17. For 'When I Set Out for Lyonnesse', see Note 10 in Chapter I above. Hardy himself had a high opinion of this poem, and was disappointed when little notice was taken of it upon its publication in 1914. Some time later he wrote to a friend : 'I learn from American newspapers that the verses "When I set out for Lyonnesse" have become quite well known in the United States and much quoted. . . . Not a soul in England . . . has thought anything of them, so far as I know.' Time has, however, served to correct that earlier neglect, and composers have allied themselves with critics to make this poem better known. In fact, no lines of Hardy's have been more frequently set to music than have the lines of this poem. Four of these settings had been published by the time of Hardy's death in 1928 ; but since his death, six other composers have chosen these lines for their compositions. On 19 October 1958 all ten settings were presented to an audience at Colby College, Waterville, Maine, U.S.A., by two members of the New

England Conservatory of Music : Lucien Olivier, baritone, and Roland Nadeau, pianist. Since the ten compositions have never been listed together (except on the programme printed for the occasion in 1958), the names of the composers and the dates of publication (or, if unpublished, the dates of composition) are given here :

1. Charles A. Speyer : London, Schott & Co.,   1920
2. C. Armstrong :   1921
3. Rutland Boughton : London, Joseph Williams,   1926
4. Frederic Austin : London, Boosey & Co.,   1927
5. Sidney Harrison : London, Augener,   1929
6. Gerald Finzi : London, Boosey & Hawkes,   1936
7. Christopher LeFleming :   *circa* 1938
8. Katherine O'Brien :   1947
9. John Duke :   1950
10. Harper McKay :   1957

It is perhaps unnecessary to add that the name 'Lyonnesse' is not Hardy's invention, but the designation, in Arthurian legend, for the country fabled to have once been contiguous to Cornwall but to have long since sunk beneath the sea. Hardy uses the name as synonymous with Cornwall.

III. 'Starry Thoughts'

1. 'Ditty', p. 126. *WP* (39), *CP* (13). Arthur McDowall noted that Hardy's poetic 'perceptions again and again are those of irony', and that in 'Ditty' even love 'singularly . . . appears the sport of place and time'.
2. *Early Life*, p. 96.
3. 'Lines to a Movement in Mozart's E-Flat Symphony', p. 128. *MV* (58), *CP* (430).
4. *Early Life*, p. 103.
5. It has been reproduced in *Some Recollections*, by Emma Hardy (London, Oxford University Press, 1961), facing page 56.
6. 'Under the Waterfall', p. 129. *SC* (85), *CP* (315). Arthur McDowall calls this poem a 'charming narrative' and thinks that 'the perception and detail' in it are 'very Browningesque'.
7. 'Where the Picnic Was', p. 131. *SC* (39), *SP* (57), *CP* (336).
8. 'The Figure in the Scene', p. 132. *MV* (98), *CP* (447).
9. 'Why Did I Sketch ?', p. 133. *MV* (99), *CP* (447).
10. 'It Never Looks like Summer', p. 134. *MV* (162), *CP* (477).
11. 'Self-Unconscious', p. 135. *SC* (77), *CP* (311). When Hardy was asked by Vere H. Collins what difference it would have

made 'if he had known', Hardy replied : 'If he had realized, when young, what he was, he would have acted differently. That is the tragedy of youth : when we know, it is too late to alter things.'

12. 'The Sun on the Bookcase', p. 137. *SC* (19), *SP* (16), *CP* (293).

13. 'The Minute Before Meeting', p. 138. *TL* (86), *CP* (219). J. E. Barton thinks that some of the lines in this poem 'are lines which Shakespeare forgot to write in one of his sonnets'.

14. 'In the Seventies', p. 139. *MV* (60), *CP* (430).

15. *Some Recollections*, by Emma Hardy, p. 34.

16. *Some Recollections*, pp. 37, 45, 46.

17. *Some Recollections*, p. 18.

18. 'I Rose and Went to Rou'tor Town', p. 140. *MV* (183), *CP* (486). When Vere Collins asked Hardy what was 'the evil wrought at Rou'tor Town', Hardy replied : 'Slander, or something of that sort'.

19. 'Near Lanivet, 1872', p. 141. *MV* (18), *CP* (409). Hardy had a high opinion of these verses. He once remarked to Vere Collins : 'This is a poem which is often neglected'. There is nothing in it to identify 'I' and 'she', but Hardy's letter of 18 January 1918 to Edmund Gosse leaves no doubt about these lines : 'You knew my late wife, and the scene occurred between us before our marriage'.

20. 'The Change', p. 143. *MV* (51), *CP* (426).

21. 'The Place on the Map', p. 145. *SC* (37), *CP* (302).

IV. THE YELLOWING LEAF

1. For Hardy's report of the gloom that 'came over the dinner', see 'At a Fashionable Dinner', p. 146. *HS* (24), *CP* (674).

2. 'We Sat at the Window', p. 147. *MV* (4), *CP* (402).

3. 'The Rift', p. 148. *LL* (126), *CP* (589).

4. 'Once at Swanage', p. 149. *HS* (178), *CP* (745).

5. 'A Two-Years' Idyll', p. 150. *LL* (139), *CP* (594).

6. 'Overlooking the River Stour', p. 151. *MV* (109), *CP* (452).

7. 'The Musical Box', p. 152. *MV* (111), *CP* (453). Arthur McDowall selected this as very 'characteristically' a Hardy poem. 'All, indeed, of this slowly moving lyric, precise in its evocation, is in his manner.'

8. 'A January Night (1879)', p. 154. *MV* (77), *CP* (438).

V. 'Our Own New-Builded Door'

1. 'Everything Comes [to him who waits]', p. 155. *MV* (163), *CP* (477). Three years after Hardy had published this poem reminiscent of 'those days' when Emma 'had nothing to pleasure her' at Max Gate, her successor (the second Mrs. Hardy) was heard to remark : 'This place is too depressing for words in the winter, when the dead leaves stick on the window-pane and the wind moans and the sky is grey and you can't even see as far as the high road'.

2. 'The Tree and the Lady', p. 156. *MV* (209), *CP* (499).

3. 'Fetching Her', p. 157. *LL* (157), *CP* (602).

4. See '*Dearest Emmie*' (1963), Letter No. 1.

5. *Hardy of Wessex* (1940), p. 165.

6. *Hardy of Wessex*, p. 164.

7. 'The Self-Unseeing', p. 158. *PP* (211), *CP* (152).

VI. 'Our Deep Division'

1. *Hardy and the Lady from Madison Square* (1952), p. 110.

2. The photograph has been reproduced in *Hardy of Wessex* (New York, 1940 ; Hamden, Connecticut, 1962), where it faces p. 174.

3. *Hardy and the Lady from Madison Square*, p. 72.

4. See '*Dearest Emmie*' (1963), p. 23.

5. *Hardy of Wessex*, pp. 167-168.

6. *Thomas Hardy: A Bibliographical Study*, by Richard Little Purdy, Oxford University Press, 1954, p. 141.

7. 'The Division', p.159. *TL* (55), *SP* (28), *CP* (205). On 5 December 1949 Siegfried Sassoon wrote to Sir Sydney Cockerell : "The Division" . . . obviously refers to Emma'.

8. 'Had You Wept', p. 160. *SC* (167), *CP* (357).

9. 'Without, Not Within Her', p. 161. *LL* (179), *CP* (612).

10. 'I Look into My Glass', p. 162. *WP* (227), *SP* (106), *CP* (72).

11. 'Memory and I', p. 163. *PP* (256), *CP* (170).

12. 'You Were the Sort that Men Forget', p. 165. *MV* (16), *CP* (408). Arthur McDowall speaks of this poem as 'real in the discernment of its feeling'.

13. *Hardy of Wessex*, p. 167.

14. William Lyon Phelps, *Autobiography*, Oxford University Press (1939), p. 391.

15. *Hardy and the Lady from Madison Square*, p. 57.

16. The *Diary* of Josephine Preston Peabody : Boston, Houghton Mifflin, 1925, p. 207.

17. *Kenneth Grahame*, by Peter Green : London, John Murray, 1959, p. 220. Quoted by permission of Miss Irene Cooper Willis.

VII. 'DAGGERS OF DISTRESS'

1. 'I Said to Love', p. 166. *PP* (75), *CP* (103).
2. 'Lost Love', p. 167. *SC* (30), *SP* (56), *CP* (299).
3. 'I Thought, my Heart', p. 168. *MV* (173), *CP* (481).
4. *Hardy of Wessex*, p. 170.
5. 'The End of the Episode', p. 169. *TL* (67), *CP* (211).
6. 'Tolerance', p. 170. *SC* (81), *CP* (313).
7. 'The Wound', p. 171. *SP* (31), *MV* (73), *CP* (436).
8. See *'Dearest Emmie'* (1963), pp. 66–90.
9. 'When Oats Were Reaped', p. 172. *HS* (152), *CP* (734).
10. See *'Dearest Emmie'* (1963), p. 91.
11. See 'The End of the Episode', p. 169, and see note 5 above.
12. See *Hardy and the Lady from Madison Square* (1952), p. 186.

VIII. 'THE STRANGE HOUSE'

1. 'Read by Moonlight', p. 173. *LL* (27), *CP* (543).
2. 'The Last Performance', p. 174. *MV* (119), *CP* (457).
3. 'The Peace-Offering', p. 175. *MV* (71), *CP* (435).
4. 'An Upbraiding', p. 176. *MV* (211), *CP* (500).
5. 'Penance', p. 177. *LL* (143), *CP* (596).
6. 'I Look in Her Face', p. 178. *LL* (145), *CP* (597).
7. 'The Prophetess', p. 179. *WW* (8), *CP* (799).
8. 'The Strange House', p. 180. *LL* (40), *CP* (549). Seven months after the publication of this poem in which Hardy spoke of hearing 'the piano playing — Just as a ghost might play', he assumed the rôle of the ghost himself. The second Mrs. Hardy was seated in the dining-room, writing ; it was 17 December 1922, just a week before Christmas Eve. She wrote : 'Ghostly strains now reach me from the drawing room — T. H. playing a Christmas hymn, on that most pathetic old piano.'
9. 'The Walk', p. 182. *SC* (99), *CP* (320). Of this poem Arthur McDowall remarks that the 'colloquial measure, with its little

flow and staccato, has its just-heard cadence that accents each turn of the mood'.

10. 'Your Last Drive', p. 183. *SC* (97), *CP* (319).
11. 'Best Times', p. 184. *LL* (256), *CP* (646).

IX. 'THE GOING'

1. 'The Going', p. 185. *SC* (95), *SP* (59), *CP* (318).
2. 'Without Ceremony', p. 187. *SC* (104), *SP* (63), *CP* (323).
3. 'Days to Recollect', p. 188. *HS* (237), *CP* (771).
4. 'A Circular', p. 189. *SC* (112), *CP* (327).
5. 'Two Lips', p. 190. *HS* (80), *CP* (699).
6. 'The Last Time', p. 191. *LL* (265), *CP* (650).
7. 'A Leaving', p. 192. *HS* (276), *CP* (790).
8. *Hardy and the Lady from Madison Square*, p. 165.
9. *Ibid.* p. 187.
10. 'Rain on a Grave', p. 193. *SC* (100), *CP* (321).
11. 'My Spirit Will Not Haunt the Mound', p. 195. *SC* (31), *SP* (76), *CP* (299).
12. 'I Found Her Out There', p. 196. *SC* (102), *SP* (61), *CP* (322). In these lines McDowall notes 'the sea-like sound and gradually closer touches of the rhythmical'.
13. 'The Riddle', p. 198. *MV* (38), *CP* (420).
14. 'Louie', p. 199. *HS* (153), *CP* (734).
15. 'The Dream is — Which ?', p. 200. *LL* (186), *CP* (615).
16. 'Lament', p. 201. *SC* (105), *CP* (323). This poem is singled out for special praise by J. E. Barton. In a number of Hardy's poems, so he declares, 'the thrill of grief is raised to monumental beauty. Several poems of the series dated 1912–13 have this character. The poem called "Lament", realistic in detail, is supremely felt, most dignified, and strikes not a note of stressed or false pathos.' (J. E. Barton, 'The Poetry of Thomas Hardy', in *The Art of Thomas Hardy*, by Lionel Johnson : New York, Dodd, Mead, 1923, p. 275.)
17. 'The Curtains Now Are Drawn', p. 203. *LL* (19), *CP* (540).
18. 'Something Tapped', p. 204. *MV* (72), *CP* (436).
19. 'The Voice', p. 205. *SC* (109), *SP* (64), *CP* (325). In this poem Hardy was deliberately using a rhythm he very rarely used — dactylic. But he knew what he was doing, and he would not wish a reader to mangle his dactylic tetrameter lines into something else. This calls for emphasis in view of

the hodge-podge of trochees and iambs proposed by Arthur
McDowall's scansion of this poem (see page 254 of his 1931
critical study *Thomas Hardy*). The poet's triple rhymes —
'listlessness — wistlessness ; call to me — all to me ; view you
then — knew you then' — are all dactylic ; and Hardy's scorn
for those who fail to note this waltz rhythm may be surmised
by recalling his words in *Later Years* (p. 79) : '. . . in . . .
the reviewer's ignorance of . . . the metre . . . [he] . . .
has tried to scan the author's sapphics as heroics'. When
Hardy wrote dactyls he wanted them read as dactyls. In the
last four lines of the poem, the rhythm of course changes, in
perfect keeping with the intensified emotion expressed.
Throughout the poem, the metrical technique is handled with
consummate appropriateness and skill. In spite of McDowall's
failure to scan the dactyls correctly, he did sense that the 'triple
rhythm must have lurked in the head of the poet who as a
boy had fiddled at country dances'. McDowall even quotes
Hardy's words (elsewhere) : 'And lightly dance some triple-
timed romance'. What misled him here, apparently, was his
noticing 'the unexpected turns of variation that Hardy gave
to any rhythm he choose', as in the last four lines of 'The
Voice'.

20. 'When Dead', p. 206. *HS* (47), *CP* (683). 'Truth and tenderness show all the plainer for the crispness of "When Dead".
It is a deeply and generously human little poem, and a light
upon all of them.' (Arthur McDowall, *Thomas Hardy : A
Critical Study*, London, Faber, 1931, pp. 267-268.)

21. 'The Prospect', p. 207. *HS* (147), *CP* (732).

22. 'End of the Year 1912', p. 208. *LL* (90), *CP* (573).

X. 'VETERIS VESTIGIA FLAMMAE'

1. 'Old Excursions', p. 209. *MV* (189), *CP* (489).

2. This line, and the poem from which it is taken, 'A Dream or
No', have already been noticed in Chapter II (see note 7 to
that chapter). The entire poem is given on p. 114.

3. 'Looking at a Picture on an Anniversary', p. 210. *MV* (213),
CP (501).

4. 'Joys of Memory', p. 211. *MV* (20), *CP* (410).

5. 'Beeny Cliff', p. 117. See Chapter II, note 9.

6. 'After a Journey', p. 212. *SC* (115), *SP* (67), *CP* (328).

7. G. M. Young, p. xv in 'Introduction' to *Selected Poems of
Thomas Hardy*, London, Macmillan, 1940.

8. 'The Haunter', p. 214. *SC* (107), *CP* (324). In this poem, says Arthur McDowall, Hardy 'invests a loved and lost companion with a tranquil and invisible spell. His truest ghosts are not wraiths but evocations.'

9. See *'Dearest Emmie'* (1963), Letter 55.

10. 'The West-of-Wessex Girl', p. 215. *LL* (23), *CP* (542).

11. 'Places', p. 120. See Chapter II, note 11.

12. 'The Marble-Streeted Town', p. 216. *LL* (251), *CP* (644).

13. 'The Clock of the Years', p. 217. *MV* (204), *CP* (496).

14. 'His Visitor', p. 218. *SC* (110), *CP* (326).

15. 'The Spell of the Rose', p. 219. *SC* (88), *CP* (334).

16. 'Paths of Former Time', p. 221. *MV* (201), *CP* (496).

17. 'This Summer and Last', p. 222. *HS* (252), *CP* (779).

18. 'A Forgotten Miniature', p. 223. *WW* (140), *CP* (858).

19. 'On a Discovered Curl of Hair', p. 224. *LL* (226), *CP* (632).

20. See Carroll A. Wilson's *Descriptive Catalogue of the Grolier Club Centenary Exhibition of the Works of Thomas Hardy* (Waterville, Maine : Colby College Library, 1940), p. 13. The locket, hair, and miniature are shown in a picture facing page 12 of this catalogue.

21. 'A Death-Day Recalled', p. 225. *SC* (117), *CP* (329).

22. 'A Night in November', p. 226. *LL* (50), *CP* (555). In this poem Arthur McDowall notices 'the quietest softness, suffusing the feeling and the tune'.

23. *Hardy of Wessex*, p. 173.

24. 'At the Piano', p. 227. *MV* (205), *CP* (497).

25. 'On the Doorstep', p. 228. *MV* (198), *CP* (494).

26. 'A Woman Driving', p. 229. *LL* (252), *CP* (645).

27. 'The Shadow on the Stone', p. 230. *MV* (206), *CP* (498).

28. 'The Marble Tablet', p. 231. *LL* (198), *CP* (620). The inscription composed by Hardy reads : 'To the dear Memory of Emma Lavinia Hardy, born Gifford, the wife of Thomas Hardy, author, and sister-in-law of the Rev. C. Holder, formerly incumbent of this parish : before her marriage she lived at the Rectory 1868–1873, conducted the church music, and laid the first stone of the re-built aisle and tower ; she died at Dorchester 1912, and is buried at Stinsford, Dorset. Erected by her husband 1913.'

29. 'The Monument-Maker', p. 232. *HS* (15), *CP* (671).

30. 'Her Haunting-Ground', p. 233. *HS* (233), *CP* (770).

31. 'He Prefers Her Earthly', p. 234. *MV* (139), *CP* (466).

32. 'If You had Known', p. 235. *LL* (148), *CP* (598). Of this poem Arthur McDowall remarks : 'The actor's ignorance is a theme of classic irony . . . but . . . in . . . "If You had Known" a purely tragic or wistful tone maintains itself'.

33. 'The Seven Times', p. 236. *LL* (266), *CP* (650).

34. 'Ten Years Since', p. 238. *HS* (49), *CP* (685).

35. 'She Opened the Door', p. 239. *HS* (154), *CP* (735).

HARDY'S LOVE POEMS

A NOTE ON THE ARRANGEMENT OF THE
POEMS IN THE PRESENT VOLUME

HARDY'S poems to and about his first wife were scattered through eight volumes published over a period of thirty years. Seven of the volumes appeared during his life ; one was posthumous. This dispersal of the poems may be summarized thus :

In *Wessex Poems* (1898)	2 poems
Poems of the Past and the Present (1902)	3 ,,
Time's Laughingstocks (1909)	3 ,,
Satires of Circumstance, Lyrics, and Reveries (1914)	32 ,,
Moments of Vision (1917)	33 ,,
Late Lyrics and Earlier (1922)	25 ,,
Human Shows, Far Phantasies (1925)	16 ,,
Winter Words (1928)	2 ,,
	116 poems

It may be of some interest to note in passing that Hardy included fourteen of these love poems in *Selected Poems* (1916) and that in *Chosen Poems* (1929) twelve of the fourteen *Selected* titles were retained.

Fifty years have passed since Hardy talked with A. C. Benson about his 'Poems of 1912-13' but throughout this half-century no attempt has been made to associate those poems closely and logically with the many others inspired by Emma Lavinia Gifford Hardy. In the *Collected Poems* all these memorial or autobiographical verses appear in the same order in which they were originally published. But that order of original publication is meaningless. For example, 'On a Discovered Curl of Hair' was published in 1922, whereas 'A Forgotten Miniature' was not published until 1928 after Hardy's death. In *Collected Poems* they are separated by 226 pages. Yet the two poems belong together ; they are accordingly placed together in this volume. The 'discovery' of the locket that contained both the curl and the miniature was made in 1913, and these two poems are therefore assigned here to that place in our order which is determined by the 1913 date.

Moreover, the order or arrangement suggested by the date of composition is almost equally meaningless, partly because of Hardy's habit of often retaining his manuscripts for a long time before publishing them, and partly because of his habit of revising at a later date a poem begun at a much earlier time. For example, 'The Figure in the Scene', published in 1917, was written after 1912 but designated as having been composed 'from an old note'; and 'The Wind's Prophecy', with its allusions to 1870, was 're-written from an old copy', and then textually revised again *after* its publication in 1917.

In the present volume, therefore, the poems are presented in a wholly new arrangement. The order parallels that of Hardy's own experience. This chronological, or biographical, arrangement is the only one that can give proper emphasis to the fact that these poems are (as Arthur McDowall pointed out) the result of 'a profoundly real experience'. McDowall was, of course, speaking primarily about the 'Poems of 1912–13', but what he had to say (p. 232) can be applied to all the poems about Emma, for they

> condense almost every quality of Hardy's verse except the sardonic, and most, if not all, of his directest utterances of feeling : passion and tenderness, memory and regret, romance and realism. They are central among the poems. . . . Almost any one of them, by itself, might take its place among the others, but they cling together with the unity and veracity of a profoundly real experience. Nowhere else, indeed, are the poet and the man so completely one as in these intimate lyrics.

Nowhere else among all of Hardy's poems would he have been able with such truthfulness and such accuracy to quote Walt Whitman's familiar words : 'Who touches this book touches a man'.

A reading of the poems in the order in which they are here presented will, then, give a clearer picture of the poet's experience than has previously been easily available to the reader. Thirteen per cent of Hardy's total poetic output deals with Emma Lavinia Gifford, but never before has the reader been able to read this part of the poetry without the intrusion of the other eighty-seven per cent and the distractions attendant upon such intrusion.

It goes without saying that the consecutive reading of these love poems will also provide the reader with a clearer picture of Mrs. Hardy, and that greater clarity will, in turn, react to permit a more appreciative reading of the poems. 'You knew my late wife,' Hardy once wrote to his friend Edmund Gosse. The implication was that acquaintance with Emma was — if not an absolute prerequisite for an understanding of the poetry — at least a help toward a greater appreciation of Hardy's verse. The present arrangement of the poems parallels the chronological sequence of the introduction ; together, they give the reader all the information he needs about the woman of whom Thomas Hardy remarked : 'She opened the door of romance to me'.

1. 'WHEN I SET OUT FOR LYONNESSE'

When I set out for Lyonnesse,
    A hundred miles away,
    The rime was on the spray,
And starlight lit my lonesomeness
When I set out for Lyonnesse
    A hundred miles away.

What would bechance at Lyonnesse
    While I should sojourn there
    No prophet durst declare,
Nor did the wisest wizard guess
What would bechance at Lyonnesse
    While I should sojourn there.

When I came back from Lyonnesse
    With magic in my eyes,
    All marked with mute surmise
My radiance rare and fathomless,
When I came back from Lyonnesse
    With magic in my eyes !

2. THE WIND'S PROPHECY

I travel on by barren farms,
And gulls glint out like silver flecks
Against a cloud that speaks of wrecks,
And bellies down with black alarms.
I say : 'Thus from my lady's arms
I go ; those arms I love the best!'
The wind replies from dip and rise,
'Nay ; toward her arms thou journeyest.'

A distant verge morosely gray
Appears, while clots of flying foam
Break from its muddy monochrome,
And a light blinks up far away.
I sigh : 'My eyes now as all day
Behold her ebon loops of hair!'
Like bursting bonds the wind responds,
'Nay, wait for tresses flashing fair!'

From tides the lofty coastlands screen
Come smitings like the slam of doors,
Or hammerings on hollow floors,
As the swell cleaves through caves unseen.
Say I : 'Though broad this wild terrene,
Her city home is matched of none!'
From the hoarse skies the wind replies :
'Thou shouldst have said her sea-bord one.'

The all-prevailing clouds exclude
The one quick timorous transient star ;
The waves outside where breakers are
Huzza like a mad multitude.
'Where the sun ups it, mist-imbued,'
I cry, 'there reigns the star for me!'
The wind outshrieks from points and peaks :
'Here, westward, where it downs, mean ye!'

Yonder the headland, vulturine,
Snores like old Skrymer in his sleep,
And every chasm and every steep
Blackens as wakes each pharos-shine.
'I roam, but one is safely mine,'
I say. 'God grant she stay my own!'
Low laughs the wind as if it grinned :
'Thy Love is one thou'st not yet known.'

On that gray night of mournful drone,
Apart from aught to hear, to see,
I dreamt not that from shires unknown
     In gloom, alone,
     By Halworthy,
A man was drawing near to me.

I'd no concern at anything,
No sense of coming pull-heart play ;
Yet, under the silent outspreading
     Of even's wing
     Where Otterham lay,
A man was riding up my way.

I thought of nobody — not of one,
But only of trifles — legends, ghosts —
Though, on the moorland dim and dun
     That travellers shun
     About these coasts,
The man had passed Tresparret Posts.

There was no light at all inland,
Only the seaward pharos-fire,
Nothing to let me understand
     That hard at hand
     By Hennett Byre
The man was getting nigh and nigher.

There was a rumble at the door,
A draught disturbed the drapery,
And but a minute passed before
     With gaze that bore
     My destiny,
The man revealed himself to me.

4. THE DISCOVERY

I wandered to a crude coast
    Like a ghost ;
Upon the hills I saw fires —
    Funeral pyres
Seemingly — and heard breaking
Waves like distant cannonades that set the land shaking.

And so I never once guessed
    A Love-nest,
Bowered and candle-lit, lay
    In my way,
Till I found a hid hollow,
Where I burst on her my heart could not but follow.

5. ST. LAUNCE'S REVISITED

Slip back, Time !
Yet again I am nearing
Castle and keep, uprearing
    Gray, as in my prime.

At the inn
Smiling nigh, why is it
Not as on my visit
    When hope and I were twin ?

Groom and jade
Whom I found here, moulder ;
Strange the tavern-holder,
    Strange the tap-maid.

Here I hired
Horse and man for bearing
Me on my wayfaring
    To the door desired.

Evening gloomed
As I journeyed forward
To the faces shoreward,
    Till their dwelling loomed.

If again
Towards the Atlantic sea there
I should speed, they'd be there
    Surely now as then ? . . .

Why waste thought,
When I know them vanished
Under earth ; yea, banished
    Ever into nought !

6. GREEN SLATES

(Penpethy)

It happened once, before the duller
    Loomings of life defined them,
I searched for slates of greenish colour
    A quarry where men mined them ;

And saw, the while I peered around there,
    In the quarry standing
A form against the slate background there,
    Of fairness eye-commanding,

And now, though fifty years have flown me,
    With all their dreams and duties,
And strange-pipped dice my hand has thrown me,
    And dust are all her beauties,

Green slates — seen high on roofs, or lower
    In waggon, truck, or lorry —
Cry out : 'Our home was where you saw her
    Standing in the quarry !'

As I drive to the junction of lane and highway,
   And the drizzle bedrenches the waggonette,
I look behind at the fading byway,
   And see on its slope, now glistening wet,
      Distinctly yet

Myself and a girlish form benighted
   In dry March weather.   We climb the road
Beside a chaise.   We had just alighted
   To ease the sturdy pony's load
      When he sighed and slowed.

What we did as we climbed, and what we talked of
   Matters not much, nor to what it led, —
Something that life will not be balked of
   Without rude reason till hope is dead,
      And feeling fled.

It filled but a minute.   But was there ever
   A time of such quality, since or before,
In that hill's story ?   To one mind never,
   Though it has been climbed, foot-swift, foot-sore,
      By thousands more.

Primaeval rocks form the road's steep border,
   And much have they faced there, first and last,
Of the transitory in Earth's long order ;
   But what they record in colour and cast
      Is — that we two passed.

And to me, though Time's unflinching rigour,
   In mindless rote, has ruled from sight
The substance now, one phantom figure
   Remains on the slope, as when that night
      Saw us alight.

I look and see it there, shrinking, shrinking,
   I look back at it amid the rain
For the very last time ; for my sand is sinking,
   And I shall traverse old love's domain
      Never again.

Why go to Saint-Juliot ?   What's Juliot to me ?
    Some strange necromancy
    But charmed me to fancy
That much of my life claims the spot as its key.

Yes.   I have had dreams of that place in the West,
    And a maiden abiding
    Thereat as in hiding ;
Fair-eyed and white-shouldered, broad-browed and brown-
    tressed.

And of how, coastward bound on a night long ago,
    There lonely I found her,
    The sea-birds around her,
And other than nigh things uncaring to know.

So sweet her life there (in my thought has it seemed)
    That quickly she drew me
    To take her unto me,
And lodge her long years with me.   Such have I dreamed.

But nought of that maid from Saint-Juliot I see ;
    Can she ever have been here,
    And shed her life's sheen here,
The woman I thought a long housemate with me ?

Does there even a place like Saint-Juliot exist ?
    Or a Vallency Valley
    With stream and leafed alley,
Or Beeny, or Bos with its flounce flinging mist ?

9. A DUETTIST TO HER PIANOFORTE

SONG OF SILENCE
(E. L. H. — H. C. H.)

Since every sound moves memories,
     How can I play you
Just as I might if you raised no scene,
By your ivory rows, of a form between
My vision and your time-worn sheen,
     As when each day you
Answered our fingers with ecstasy ?
So it's hushed, hushed, hushed, you are for me !

And I am doomed to counterchord
     Her notes no more
In those old things I used to know,
In a fashion, when we practised so,
'Good-night ! — Good-bye !' to your pleated show
     Of silk, now hoar,
Each nodding hammer, and pedal and key,
For dead, dead, dead, you are to me !

I fain would second her, strike to her stroke,
     As when she was by,
Aye, even from the ancient clamorous 'Fall
Of Paris,' or 'Battle of Prague' withal,
To the 'Roving Minstrels,' or 'Elfin Call'
     Sung soft as a sigh :
But upping ghosts press achefully,
And mute, mute, mute, you are for me !

Should I fling your polyphones, plaints, and quavers
    Afresh on the air,
Too quick would the small white shapes be here
Of the fellow twain of hands so dear ;
And a black-tressed profile, and pale smooth ear ;
    — Then how shall I bear
Such heavily-haunted harmony ?
Nay : hushed, hushed, hushed, you are for me !

10. BEENY CLIFF

O the opal and the sapphire of that wandering western sea,
And the woman riding high above with bright hair flapping
free —
The woman whom I loved so, and who loyally loved me.

The pale mews plained below us, and the waves seemed far
away
In a nether sky, engrossed in saying their ceaseless babbling
say,
As we laughed light-heartedly aloft on that clear-sunned
March day.

A little cloud then cloaked us, and there flew an irised rain,
And the Atlantic dyed its levels with a dull misfeatured stain,
And then the sun burst out again, and purples prinked the
main.

— Still in all its chasmal beauty bulks old Beeny to the sky,
And shall she and I not go there once again now March is
nigh,
And the sweet things said in that March say anew there by
and by ?

What if still in chasmal beauty looms that wild weird western
shore,
The woman now is — elsewhere — whom the ambling pony
bore,
And nor knows nor cares for Beeny, and will laugh there
nevermore.

Queer are the ways of a man I know :
        He comes and stands
        In a careworn craze,
        And looks at the sands
        And the seaward haze
        With moveless hands
        And face and gaze,
        Then turns to go . . .
And what does he see when he gazes so ?

They say he sees as an instant thing
        More clear than to-day,
        A sweet soft scene
        That was once in play
        By that briny green ;
        Yes, notes alway
        Warm, real, and keen,
        What his back years bring —
A phantom of his own figuring.

Of this vision of his they might say more :
        Not only there
        Does he see this sight,
        But everywhere
        In his brain — day, night,
        As if on the air
        It were drawn rose-bright —
        Yea, far from that shore
Does he carry this vision of heretofore :

A ghost-girl-rider. And though, toil-tried,
      He withers daily,
      Time touches her not,
      But she still rides gaily
      In his rapt thought
      On that shagged and shaly
      Atlantic spot,
      And as when first eyed
Draws rein and sings to the swing of the tide.

12. PLACES

Nobody says : Ah, that is the place
Where chanced, in the hollow of years ago,
What none of the Three Towns cared to know —
The birth of a little girl of grace —
The sweetest the house saw, first or last ;
      Yet it was so
      On that day long past.

Nobody thinks : There, there she lay
In a room by the Hoe, like the bud of a flower,
And listened, just after the bedtime hour,
To the stammering chimes that used to play
The quaint Old Hundred-and-Thirteenth tune
      In Saint Andrew's tower
      Night, morn, and noon.

Nobody calls to mind that here
Upon Boterel Hill, where the waggoners skid,
With cheeks whose airy flush outbid
Fresh fruit in bloom, and free of fear,
She cantered down, as if she must fall
      (Though she never did),
      To the charm of all.

Nay : one there is to whom these things,
That nobody else's mind calls back,
Have a savour that scenes in being lack,
And a presence more than the actual brings ;
To whom to-day is beneaped and stale,
      And its urgent clack
      But a vapid tale.

I have seen her in gowns the brightest,
  Of azure, green, and red,
And in the simplest, whitest,
  Muslined from heel to head ;
I have watched her walking, riding,
  Shade-flecked by a leafy tree,
Or in fixed thought abiding
  By the foam-fingered sea.

In woodlands I have known her,
  When boughs were mourning loud,
In the rain-reek she has shown her
  Wild-haired and watery-browed.
And once or twice she has cast me
  As she pomped along the street
Court-clad, ere quite she had passed me,
  A glance from her chariot-seat.

But in my memoried passion
  For evermore stands she
In the gown of fading fashion
  She wore that night when we,
Doomed long to part, assembled
  In the snug small room ; yea, when
She sang with lips that trembled,
  'Shall I see his face again ?'

14. THE FROZEN GREENHOUSE

(St. Juliot)

'There was a frost
Last night !' she said,
'And the stove was forgot
When we went to bed,
And the greenhouse plants
Are frozen dead !'

By the breakfast blaze
Blank-faced spoke she,
Her scared young look
Seeming to be
The very symbol
Of tragedy.

The frost is fiercer
Than then to-day,
As I pass the place
Of her once dismay,
But the greenhouse stands
Warm, tight, and gay,

While she who grieved
At the sad lot
Of her pretty plants —
Cold, iced, forgot —
Herself is colder,
And knows it not.

She looked like a bird from a cloud
    On the clammy lawn,
Moving alone, bare-browed
    In the dim of dawn.
The candles alight in the room
    For my parting meal
Made all things withoutdoors loom
    Strange, ghostly, unreal.

The hour itself was a ghost,
    And it seemed to me then
As of chances the chance furthermost
    I should see her again.
I beheld not where all was so fleet
    That a Plan of the past
Which had ruled us from birthtime to meet
    Was in working at last :

No prelude did I there perceive
    To a drama at all,
Or foreshadow what fortune might weave
    From beginnings so small ;
But I rose as if quicked by a spur
    I was bound to obey,
And stepped through the casement to her
    Still alone in the gray.

'I am leaving you. . . . Farewell !' I said,
    As I followed her on
By an alley bare boughs overspread ;
    'I soon must be gone !'
Even then the scale might have been turned
    Against love by a feather,
— But crimson one cheek of hers burned
    When we came in together.

16. 'AS 'TWERE TO-NIGHT'

As 'twere to-night, in the brief space
        Of a far eventime,
        My spirit rang achime
At vision of a girl of grace ;
As 'twere to-night, in the brief space
        Of a far eventime.

As 'twere at noontide of to-morrow
        I airily walked and talked,
        And wondered as I walked
What it could mean, this soar from sorrow ;
As 'twere at noontide of to-morrow
        I airily walked and talked.

As 'twere at waning of this week
        Broke a new life on me ;
        Trancings of bliss to be
In some dim dear land soon to seek ;
As 'twere at waning of this week
        Broke a new life on me !

17. A WEEK

On Monday night I closed my door,
And thought you were not as heretofore,
And little cared if we met no more.

I seemed on Tuesday night to trace
Something beyond mere commonplace
In your ideas, and heart, and face.

On Wednesday I did not opine
Your life would ever be one with mine,
Though if it were we should well combine.

On Thursday noon I liked you well,
And fondly felt that we must dwell
Not far apart, whatever befell.

On Friday it was with a thrill
In gazing towards your distant vill
I owned you were my dear one still.

I saw you wholly to my mind
On Saturday — even one who shrined
All that was best of womankind.

As wing-clipt sea-gull for the sea
On Sunday night I longed for thee,
Without whom life were waste to me !

18. DITTY

(E. L. G.)

Beneath a knap where flown
    Nestlings play,
Within walls of weathered stone,
    Far away
From the files of formal houses,
By the bough the firstling browses,
Lives a Sweet : no merchants meet,
No man barters, no man sells
    Where she dwells.

Upon that fabric fair
    'Here is she !'
Seems written everywhere
    Unto me.
But to friends and nodding neighbours,
Fellow-wights in lot and labours,
Who descry the times as I,
No such lucid legend tells
    Where she dwells.

Should I lapse to what I was
    Ere we met ;
(Such will not be, but because
    Some forget
Let me feign it) — none would notice
That where she I know by rote is
Spread a strange and withering change,
Like a drying of the wells
    Where she dwells.

To feel I might have kissed —
    Loved as true —
Otherwhere, nor Mine have missed
    My life through,
Had I never wandered near her,
Is a smart severe — severer
In the thought that she is nought,
Even as I, beyond the dells
    Where she dwells.

And Devotion droops her glance
    To recall
What bond-servants of Chance
    We are all.
I but found her in that, going
On my errant path unknowing,
I did not out-skirt the spot
That no spot on earth excels,
    — Where she dwells !

19. LINES

To a Movement in Mozart's E-Flat Symphony

Show me again the time
When in the Junetide's prime
We flew by meads and mountains northerly ! —
Yea, to such freshness, fairness, fulness, fineness, freeness,
Love lures life on.

Show me again the day
When from the sandy bay
We looked together upon the pestered sea ! —
Yea, to such surging, swaying, sighing, swelling, shrinking,
Love lures life on.

Show me again the hour
When by the pinnacled tower
We eyed each other and feared futurity ! —
Yea, to such bodings, broodings, beatings, blanchings, bless-
ings,
Love lures life on.

Show me again just this :
The moment of that kiss
Away from the prancing folk, by the strawberry-tree ! —
Yea, to such rashness, ratheness, rareness, ripeness, richness,
Love lures life on.

20. UNDER THE WATERFALL

'Whenever I plunge my arm, like this,
In a basin of water, I never miss
The sweet sharp sense of a fugitive day
Fetched back from its thickening shroud of gray.
     Hence the only prime
     And real love-rhyme
     That I know by heart,
     And that leaves no smart,
Is the purl of a little valley fall
About three spans wide and two spans tall
Over a table of solid rock,
And into a scoop of the self-same block ;
The purl of a runlet that never ceases
In stir of kingdoms, in wars, in peaces ;
With a hollow boiling voice it speaks
And has spoken since hills were turfless peaks.'

'And why gives this the only prime
Idea to you of a real love-rhyme ?
And why does plunging your arm in a bowl
Full of spring water, bring throbs to your soul ?'

'Well, under the fall, in a crease of the stone,
Though where precisely none ever has known,
Jammed darkly, nothing to show how prized,
And by now with its smoothness opalized,
     Is a drinking-glass :
     For, down that pass
     My lover and I
     Walked under a sky
Of blue with a leaf-wove awning of green,
In the burn of August, to paint the scene,
And we placed our basket of fruit and wine

By the runlet's rim, where we sat to dine ;
And when we had drunk from the glass together,
Arched by the oak-copse from the weather,
I held the vessel to rinse in the fall,
Where it slipped, and sank, and was past recall,
Though we stooped and plumbed the little abyss
With long bared arms.   There the glass still is.
And, as said, if I thrust my arm below
Cold water in basin or bowl, a throe
From the past awakens a sense of that time,
And the glass we used, and the cascade's rhyme.
The basin seems the pool, and its edge
The hard smooth face of the brook-side ledge,
And the leafy pattern of china-ware
The hanging plants that were bathing there.

'By night, by day, when it shines or lours,
There lies intact that chalice of ours,
And its presence adds to the rhyme of love
Persistently sung by the fall above.
No lip has touched it since his and mine
In turns therefrom sipped lovers' wine.'

21. WHERE THE PICNIC WAS

Where we made the fire
In the summer time
Of branch and briar
On the hill to the sea,
I slowly climb
Through winter mire,
And scan and trace
The forsaken place
Quite readily.

Now a cold wind blows,
And the grass is gray,
But the spot still shows
As a burnt circle — aye,
And stick-ends, charred,
Still strew the sward
Whereon I stand,
Last relic of the band
Who came that day !

Yes, I am here
Just as last year,
And the sea breathes brine
From its strange straight line
Up hither, the same
As when we four came.
— But two have wandered far
From this grassy rise
Into urban roar,
Where no picnics are,
And one — has shut her eyes
For evermore.

22. THE FIGURE IN THE SCENE

It pleased her to step in front and sit
    Where the cragged slope was green,
While I stood back that I might pencil it
    With her amid the scene ;
        Till it gloomed and rained ;
But I kept on, despite the drifting wet
    That fell and stained
My draught, leaving for curious quizzings yet
    The blots engrained.

And thus I drew her there alone,
    Seated amid the gauze
Of moisture, hooded, only her outline shown,
    With rainfall marked across.
        — Soon passed our stay ;
Yet her rainy form is the Genius still of the spot,
    Immutable, yea,
Though the place now knows her no more, and has
    known her not
        Ever since that day.

23. 'WHY DID I SKETCH'

Why did I sketch an upland green,
    And put the figure in
    Of one on the spot with me ? —
For now that one has ceased to be seen
    The picture waxes akin
    To a wordless irony.

If you go drawing on down or cliff
    Let no soft curves intrude
    Of a woman's silhouette,
But show the escarpments stark and stiff
    As in utter solitude ;
    So shall you half forget.

Let me sooner pass from sight of the sky
    Than again on a thoughtless day
    Limn, laugh, and sing, and rhyme
With a woman sitting near, whom I
    Paint in for love, and who may
    Be called hence in my time !

24. 'IT NEVER LOOKS LIKE SUMMER'

'It never looks like summer here
    On Beeny by the sea.'
But though she saw its look as drear,
    Summer it seemed to me.

It never looks like summer now
    Whatever weather's there ;
But ah, it cannot anyhow,
    On Beeny or elsewhere !

BOSCASTLE
  March 8, 1913

25. SELF-UNCONSCIOUS

Along the way
He walked that day,
Watching shapes that reveries limn,
And seldom he
Had eyes to see
The moment that encompassed him.

Bright yellowhammers
Made mirthful clamours,
And billed long straws with a bustling air,
And bearing their load
Flew up the road
That he followed, alone, without interest there.

From bank to ground
And over and round
They sidled along the adjoining hedge ;
Sometimes to the gutter
Their yellow flutter
Would dip from the nearest slatestone ledge.

The smooth sea-line
With a metal shine,
And flashes of white, and a sail thereon,
He would also descry
With a half-wrapt eye
Between the projects he mused upon.

Yes, round him were these
Earth's artistries,
But specious plans that came to his call
Did most engage
His pilgrimage,
While himself he did not see at all.

Dead now as sherds
Are the yellow birds,
And all that mattered has passed away ;
Yet God, the Elf,
Now shows him that self
As he was, and should have been shown, that day.

O it would have been good
Could he then have stood
At a clear-eyed distance, and conned the whole,
But now such vision
Is mere derision,
Nor soothes his body nor saves his soul.

Not much, some may
Incline to say,
To see therein, had it all been seen.
Nay ! he is aware
A thing was there
That loomed with an immortal mien.

Once more the cauldron of the sun
Smears the bookcase with winy red,
And here my page is, and there my bed,
And the apple-tree shadows travel along.
Soon their intangible track will be run,
  And dusk grow strong
  And they have fled.

Yes : now the boiling ball is gone,
And I have wasted another day. . . .
But wasted — *wasted*, do I say ?
Is it a waste to have imaged one
Beyond the hills there, who, anon,
  My great deeds done,
  Will be mine alway ?

27. THE MINUTE BEFORE MEETING

The grey gaunt days dividing us in twain
  Seemed hopeless hills my strength must faint to climb,
But they are gone ; and now I would detain
  The few clock-beats that part us ; rein back Time,

And live in close expectance never closed
  In change for far expectance closed at last,
So harshly has expectance been imposed
  On my long need while these slow blank months passed.

And knowing that what is now about to be
  Will all *have been* in O, so short a space !
I read beyond it my despondency
  When more dividing months shall take its place,
  Thereby denying to this hour of grace
A full-up measure of felicity.

28. 'IN THE SEVENTIES'

Qui deridetur ab amico suo sicut ego.'—Job.

In the seventies I was bearing in my breast,
        Penned tight,
Certain starry thoughts that threw a magic light
On the worktimes and the soundless hours of rest
In the seventies ; aye, I bore them in my breast
        Penned tight.

In the seventies when my neighbours — even my friend —
        Saw me pass,
Heads were shaken, and I heard the words, 'Alas,
For his onward years and name unless he mend !'
In the seventies, when my neighbours and my friend
        Saw me pass.

In the seventies those who met me did not know
        Of the vision
That immuned me from the chillings of misprision
And the damps that choked my goings to and fro
In the seventies ; yea, those nodders did not know
        Of the vision.

In the seventies nought could darken or destroy it,
        Locked in me,
Though as delicate as lamp-worm's lucency ;
Neither mist nor murk could weaken or alloy it
In the seventies ! — could not darken or destroy it,
        Locked in me.

29. 'I ROSE AND WENT TO ROU'TOR TOWN'

(She, alone)

I rose and went to Rou'tor Town
    With gaiety and good heart,
    And ardour for the start,
That morning ere the moon was down
That lit me off to Rou'tor Town
    With gaiety and good heart.

When sojourn soon at Rou'tor Town
    Wrote sorrows on my face,
    I strove that none should trace
The pale and gray, once pink and brown,
When sojourn soon at Rou'tor Town
    Wrote sorrows on my face.

The evil wrought at Rou'tor Town
    On him I'd loved so true
    I cannot tell anew :
But nought can quench, but nought can drown
The evil wrought at Rou'tor Town
    On him I'd loved so true !

There was a stunted handpost just on the crest,
    Only a few feet high :
She was tired, and we stopped in the twilight-time for her
  rest,
    At the crossways close thereby.

She leant back, being so weary, against its stem
    And laid her arms on its own,
Each open palm stretched out to each end of them,
    Her sad face sideways thrown.

Her white-clothed form at this dim-lit cease of day
    Made her look as one crucified
In my gaze at her from the midst of the dusty way,
    And hurriedly 'Don't', I cried.

I do not think she heard. Loosing thence she said,
    As she stepped forth ready to go,
'I am rested now. — Something strange came into my head,
    I wish I had not leant so !'

And wordless we moved onward down from the hill
    In the west cloud's murked obscure,
And looking back we could see the handpost still
    In the solitude of the moor.

'It struck her too,' I thought, for as if afraid
    She heavily breathed as we trailed ;
Till she said, 'I did not think how 'twould look in the shade,
    When I leant there like one nailed.'

I, lightly : 'There's nothing in it.   For *you*, anyhow !'
  — 'O I know there is not,' said she . . .
'Yet I wonder . . . If no one is bodily crucified now,
  In spirit one may be !'

And we dragged on and on, while we seemed to see
  In the running of Time's far glass
Her crucified, as she had wondered if she might be
  Some day. — Alas, alas !

Out of the past there rises a week —
   Who shall read the years O ! —
Out of the past there rises a week
   Enringed with a purple zone.
Out of the past there rises a week
When thoughts were strung too thick to speak,
And the magic of its lineaments remains with me alone.

In that week there was heard a singing —
   Who shall spell the years, the years ! —
In that week there was heard a singing,
   And the white owl wondered why.
In that week, yea, a voice was ringing,
   And forth from the casement were candles flinging
Radiance that fell on the deodar and lit up the path
      thereby.

Could that song have a mocking note ? —
   Who shall unroll the years O ! —
Could that song have a mocking note
   To the white owl's sense as it fell ?
Could that song have a mocking note
As it trilled out warm from the singer's throat,
And who was the mocker and who the mocked when
      two felt all was well ?

In a tedious trampling crowd yet later —
   Who shall bare the years, the years ! —
In a tedious trampling crowd yet later,
   When silvery singings were dumb ;
In a crowd uncaring what time might fate her,
   Mid murks of night I stood to await her,
And the twanging of iron wheels gave out the signal
      that she was come.

She said with a travel-tired smile —
   Who shall lift the years O ! —
She said with a travel-tired smile,
   Half scared by scene so strange ;
She said, outworn by mile on mile,
The blurred lamps wanning her face the while,
'O Love, I am here ; I am with you !' . . . Ah, that
     there should have come a change !

O the doom by someone spoken —
   Who shall unseal the years, the years ! —
O the doom that gave no token,
   When nothing of bale saw we :
O the doom by someone spoken,
O the heart by someone broken,
The heart whose sweet reverberances are all time leaves
     to me.

I look upon the map that hangs by me —
Its shires and towns and rivers lined in varnished artistry —
    And I mark a jutting height
    Coloured purple, with a margin of blue sea.

— 'Twas a day of latter summer, hot and dry ;
Ay, even the waves seemed drying as we walked on, she
        and I
    By this spot where, calmly quite,
    She unfolded what would happen by and by.

This hanging map depicts the coast and place,
And re-creates therewith our unforeboded troublous case
    All distinctly to my sight,
    And her tension, and the aspect of her face.

Weeks and weeks we had loved beneath that blazing blue,
Which had lost the art of raining, as her eyes to-day had too,
    While she told what, as by sleight,
    Shot our firmament with rays of ruddy hue.

For the wonder and the wormwood of the whole
Was that what in realms of reason would have joyed our
        double soul
    Wore a torrid tragic light
    Under order-keeping's rigorous control.

So, the map revives her words, the spot, the time,
And the thing we found we had to face before the next
        year's prime ;
    The charted coast stares bright,
    And its episode comes back in pantomime.

We sat with the banqueting-party
    By the table-end —
Unmarked, — no diners out
    Were we : scarce a friend
    Of our own mind's trend
Was there, though the welcome was hearty.
Then we noticed a shade extend
    By a distant screen,
And I said : 'What to you does it seem to mean,
    Lavine ?'

'— It is like my own body lying
    Beyond the door
Where the servants glide in and about
    The carpeted floor ;
    And it means my death hour ! —'
'— What a fancy ! Who feels like dying
While these smart sallies pour,
    With laughter between !
To me it is more like satin sheen,
    Lavine.'

'— That means your new bride, when you win her :
    Yes, so it must be !
It's her satin dress, no doubt —
    That shine you see —
    My own corpse to me !'
And a gloom came over the dinner,
Where almost strangers were we,
    As the spirit of the scene
Forsook her — the fairest of the whole thirteen —
    Lavine !

34. 'WE SAT AT THE WINDOW'

(Bournemouth, 1875)

We sat at the window looking out,
And the rain came down like silken strings
That Swithin's day.   Each gutter and spout
Babbled unchecked in the busy way
    Of witless things :
Nothing to read, nothing to see
Seemed in that room for her and me
    On Swithin's day.

We were irked by the scene, by our own selves ; yes,
For I did not know, nor did she infer
How much there was to read and guess
By her in me, and to see and crown
    By me in her.
Wasted were two souls in their prime,
And great was the waste, that July time
    When the rain came down.

'Twas just at gnat and cobweb-time,
When yellow begins to show in the leaf,
That your old gamut changed its chime
From those true tones — of span so brief ! —
That met my beats of joy, of grief,
      As rhyme meets rhyme.

So sank I from my high sublime !
We faced but chancewise after that,
And never I knew or guessed my crime. . . .
Yes ; 'twas the date — or nigh thereat —
Of the yellowing leaf ; at moth and gnat
      And cobweb-time.

The spray sprang up across the cusps of the moon,
 And all its light loomed green
 As a witch-flame's weirdsome sheen
At the minute of an incantation scene ;
And it greened our gaze — that night at demilune.

Roaring high and roaring low was the sea
 Behind the headland shores :
 It symboled the slamming of doors,
Or a regiment hurrying over hollow floors. . . .
And there we two stood, hands clasped ; I and she !

Yes ; such it was ;
Just those two seasons unsought,
Sweeping like summertide wind on our ways ;
Moving, as straws,
Hearts quick as ours in those days ;
Going like wind, too, and rated as nought
Save as the prelude to plays
Soon to come — larger, life-fraught :
Yes ; such it was.

'Nought' it was called,
Even by ourselves — that which springs
Out of the years for all flesh, first or last,
Commonplace, scrawled
Dully on days that go past.
Yet, all the while, it upbore us like wings
Even in hours overcast :
Aye, though this best of things,
'Nought' it was called !

What seems it now ?
Lost : such beginning was all ;
Nothing came after : romance straight forsook
Quickly somehow
Life when we sped from our nook,
Primed for new scenes with designs smart and tall. . . .
— A preface without any book,
A trumpet unlipped, but no call ;
That seems it now.

The swallows flew in the curves of an eight
     Above the river-gleam
     In the wet June's last beam :
Like little crossbows animate
The swallows flew in the curves of an eight
     Above the river-gleam.

Planing up shavings of crystal spray
     A moor-hen darted out
     From the bank thereabout,
And through the stream-shine ripped his way ;
Planing up shavings of crystal spray
     A moor-hen darted out.

Closed were the kingcups ; and the mead
     Dripped in monotonous green,
     Though the day's morning sheen
Had shown it golden and honeybee'd ;
Closed were the kingcups ; and the mead
     Dripped in monotonous green.

And never I turned my head, alack,
     While these things met my gaze
     Through the pane's drop-drenched glaze,
To see the more behind my back. . . .
O never I turned, but let, alack,
     These less things hold my gaze.

Lifelong to be
Seemed the fair colour of the time ;
That there was standing shadowed near
A spirit who sang to the gentle chime
Of the self-struck notes, I did not hear,
    I did not see.

Thus did it sing
To the mindless lyre that played indoors
As she came to listen for me without :
'O value what the nonce outpours —
This best of life — that shines about
    Your welcoming !'

I had slowed along
After the torrid hours were done,
Though still the posts and walls and road
Flung back their sense of the hot-faced sun,
And had walked by Stourside Mill, where broad
    Stream-lilies throng.

And I descried
The dusky house that stood apart,
And her, white-muslined, waiting there
In the porch with high-expectant heart,
While still the thin mechanic air
    Went on inside.

At whiles would flit
Swart bats, whose wings, be-webbed and tanned,
Whirred like the wheels of ancient clocks :
She laughed a hailing as she scanned
Me in the gloom, the tuneful box
    Intoning it.

Lifelong to be
I thought it.   That there watched hard by
A spirit who sang to the indoor tune,
'O make the most of what is nigh !'
I did not hear in my dull soul-swoon —
I did not see.

40. A JANUARY NIGHT

The rain smites more and more,
   The east wind snarls and sneezes ;
Through the joints of the quivering door
    The water wheezes.

The tip of each ivy-shoot
   Writhes on its neighbour's face ;
There is some hid dread afoot
    That we cannot trace.

Is it the spirit astray
   Of the man at the house below
Whose coffin they took in to-day ?
    We do not know.

'The house is bleak and cold
    Built so new for me !
All the winds upon the wold
    Search it through for me ;
No screening trees abound,
And the curious eyes around,
    Keep on view for me.'

'My Love, I am planting trees
    As a screen for you
Both from winds, and eyes that tease
    And peer in for you.
Only wait till they have grown,
No such bower will be known
    As I mean for you.'

'Then I will bear it, Love,
    And will wait,' she said.
— So, with years, there grew a grove.
    'Skill how great !' she said.
'As you wished, Dear ?' — 'Yes, I see !
But — I'm dying ; and for me
    'Tis too late,' she said.

  I have done all I could
For that lady I knew ! Through the heats I have shaded her,
Drawn to her songsters when summer has jaded her,
  Home from the heath or the wood.

  At the mirth-time of May,
When my shadow first lured her, I'd donned my new bravery
Of greenth : 'twas my all. Now I shiver in slavery,
  Icicles grieving me gray.

  Plumed to every twig's end
I could tempt her chair under me. Much did I treasure her
During those days she had nothing to pleasure her ;
  Mutely she used me as friend.

  I'm a skeleton now,
And she's gone, craving warmth. The rime sticks like a skin
  to me ;
Through me Arcturus peers ; Nor'lights shoot into me ;
  Gone is she, scorning my bough !

43. FETCHING HER

An hour before the dawn,
        My friend,
You lit your waiting bedside-lamp,
  Your breakfast-fire anon,
And outing into the dark and damp
  You saddled, and set on.

Thuswise, before the day,
        My friend,
You sought her on her surfy shore,
  To fetch her thence away
Unto your own new-builded door
  For a staunch lifelong stay.

You said : 'It seems to be,
        My friend,
That I were bringing to my place
  The pure brine breeze, the sea,
The mews — all her old sky and space,
  In bringing her with me !'

— But time is prompt to expugn,
        My friend,
Such magic-minted conjurings :
  The brought breeze fainted soon,
And then the sense of seamews' wings,
  And the shore's sibilant tune.

So, it had been more due,
        My friend,
Perhaps, had you not pulled this flower
  From the craggy nook it knew,
And set it in an alien bower ;
  But left it where it grew !

Here is the ancient floor,
　　Footworn and hollowed and thin,
Here was the former door
　　Where the dead feet walked in.

She sat here in her chair,
　　Smiling into the fire ;
He who played stood there,
　　Bowing it higher and higher.

Childlike, I danced in a dream ;
　　Blessings emblazoned that day ;
Everything glowed with a gleam ;
　　Yet we were looking away !

45. THE DIVISION

Rain on the windows, creaking doors,
    With blasts that besom the green,
And I am here, and you are there,
    And a hundred miles between !

O were it but the weather, Dear,
    O were it but the miles
That summed up all our severance,
    There might be room for smiles.

But that thwart thing betwixt us twain,
    Which nothing cleaves or clears,
Is more than distance, Dear, or rain,
    And longer than the years !

Had you wept ; had you but neared me with a hazed un-
    certain ray,
Dewy as the face of the dawn, in your large and luminous
    eye,
Then would have come back all the joys the tidings had slain
    that day,
And a new beginning, a fresh fair heaven, have smoothed the
    things awry.
But you were less feebly human, and no passionate need for
    clinging
Possessed your soul to overthrow reserve when I came near ;
Ay, though you suffer as much as I from storms the hours are
    bringing
Upon your heart and mine, I never see you shed a tear.

The deep strong woman is weakest, the weak one is the
    strong ;
The weapon of all weapons best for winning, you have not
    used ;
Have you never been able, or would you not, through the
    evil times and long ?
Has not the gift been given you, or such gift have you
    refused ?
When I bade me not absolve you on that evening or the
    morrow,
Why did you not make war on me with those who weep
    like rain ?
You felt too much, so gained no balm for all your torrid
    sorrow,
And hence our deep division, and our dark undying pain.

It was what you bore with you, Woman,
    Not inly were,
That throned you from all else human,
    However fair !

It was that strange freshness you carried
    Into a soul
Whereon no thought of yours tarried
    Two moments at all.

And out from his spirit flew death,
    And bale, and ban,
Like the corn-chaff under the breath
    Of the winnowing-fan.

48. 'I LOOK INTO MY GLASS'

I look into my glass,
And view my wasting skin,
And say, 'Would God it came to pass
My heart had shrunk as thin !'

For then, I, undistrest
By hearts grown cold to me,
Could lonely wait my endless rest
With equanimity.

But Time, to make me grieve,
Part steals, lets part abide ;
And shakes this fragile frame at eve
With throbbings of noontide.

'O Memory, where is now my youth,
Who used to say that life was truth ?'

   'I saw him in a crumbled cot
     Beneath a tottering tree ;
   That he as phantom lingers there
     Is only known to me.'

'O Memory, where is now my joy,
Who lived with me in sweet employ ?'

   'I saw him in gaunt gardens lone,
     Where laughter used to be ;
   That he as phantom wanders there
     Is known to none but me.'

'O Memory, where is now my hope,
Who charged with deeds my skill and scope ?'

   'I saw her in a tomb of tomes,
     Where dreams are wont to be ;
   That she as spectre haunteth there
     Is only known to me.'

'O Memory, where is now my faith,
One time a champion, now a wraith ?'

   'I saw her in a ravaged aisle,
     Bowed down on bended knee ;
   That her poor ghost outflickers there
     Is known to none but me.'

'O Memory, where is now my love,
That rayed me as a god above ?'

    'I saw her in an ageing shape,
       Where beauty used to be ;
    That her fond phantom lingers there
       Is only known to me.'

You were the sort that men forget ;
　　Though I — not yet ! —
Perhaps not ever.　Your slighted weakness
　Adds to the strength of my regret !

You'd not the art — you never had
　　For good or bad —
To make men see how sweet your meaning,
　Which, visible, had charmed them glad.

You would, by words inept let fall,
　　Offend them all,
Even if they saw your warm devotion
　Would hold your life's blood at their call.

You lacked the eye to understand
　　Those friends offhand
Whose mode was crude, though whose dim purport
　Outpriced the courtesies of the bland.

I am now the only being who
　　Remembers you
It may be.　What a waste that Nature
　Grudged soul so dear the art its due !

51. 'I SAID TO LOVE'

I said to Love,
'It is not now as in old days
When men adored thee and thy ways
    All else above ;
Named thee the Boy, the Bright, the One
Who spread a heaven beneath the sun,'
    I said to Love.

I said to Love,
'We now know more of thee than then ;
We were but weak in judgment when,
    With hearts abrim,
We clamoured thee that thou would'st please
Inflict on us thine agonies,'
    I said to him.

I said to him,
'Thou art not young, thou art not fair,
No elfin darts, no cherub air,
    Nor swan, nor dove
Are thine ; but features pitiless,
And iron daggers of distress,'
    I said to Love.

'Depart then, Love ! . . .
— Man's race shall perish, threatenest thou,
Without thy kindling coupling-vow ?
The age to come the man of now
    Know nothing of ? —
We fear not such a threat from thee ;
We are too old in apathy !
Mankind shall cease. — So let it be,'
    I said to Love.

52. LOST LOVE

I play my sweet old airs —
    The airs he knew
    When our love was true —
    But he does not balk
    His determined walk,
And passes up the stairs.

I sing my songs once more,
    And presently hear
    His footstep near
    As if it would stay ;
    But he goes his way,
And shuts a distant door.

So I wait for another morn,
    And another night
    In this soul-sick blight ;
    And I wonder much
    As I sit, why such
A woman as I was born !

53. 'I THOUGHT, MY HEART'

I thought, my Heart, that you had healed
Of those sore smartings of the past,
And that the summers had oversealed
    All mark of them at last.
But closely scanning in the night
I saw them standing crimson-bright
        Just as she made them :
        Nothing could fade them ;
        Yea, I can swear
        That there they were —
        They still were there !

Then the Vision of her who cut them came,
And looking over my shoulder said,
'I am sure you deal me all the blame
    For those sharp smarts and red ;
But meet me, dearest, to-morrow night,
In the churchyard at the moon's half-height,
        And so strange a kiss
        Shall be mine, I wis,
        That you'll cease to know
        If the wounds you show
        Be there or no !'

Indulge no more may we
In this sweet-bitter pastime :
The love-light shines the last time
    Between you, Dear, and me.

There shall remain no trace
Of what so closely tied us,
And blank as ere love eyed us
    Will be our meeting-place.

The flowers and thymy air,
Will they now miss our coming ?
The dumbles thin their humming
    To find we haunt not there ?

Though fervent was our vow,
Though ruddily ran our pleasure,
Bliss has fulfilled its measure,
    And sees its sentence now.

Ache deep ; but make no moans :
Smile out ; but stilly suffer :
The paths of love are rougher
    Than thoroughfares of stones.

'It is a foolish thing,' said I,
'To bear with such, and pass it by ;
Yet so I do, I know not why !'

And at each cross I would surmise
That if I had willed not in that wise
I might have spared me many sighs.

But now the only happiness
In looking back that I possess —
Whose lack would leave me comfortless —

Is to remember I refrained
From masteries I might have gained,
And for my tolerance was disdained ;

For see, a tomb.   And if it were
I had bent and broke, I should not dare
To linger in the shadows there.

56. THE WOUND

I climbed to the crest,
  And, fog-festooned,
The sun lay west
  Like a crimson wound :

Like that wound of mine
  Of which none knew,
For I'd given no sign
  That it pierced me through.

57. WHEN OATS WERE REAPED

That day when oats were reaped, and wheat was ripe, and
    barley ripening,
    The road-dust hot, and the bleaching grasses dry,
      I walked along and said,
While looking just ahead to where some silent people lie :

'I wounded one who's there, and now know well I wounded
    her ;
    But, ah, she does not know that she wounded me !'
      And not an air stirred,
Nor a bill of any bird ; and no response accorded she.

I paused to read a letter of hers
 By the moon's cold shine,
Eyeing it in the tenderest way,
And edging it up to catch each ray
 Upon her light-penned line.
I did not know what years would flow
 Of her life's span and mine
Ere I read another letter of hers
 By the moon's cold shine !

I chance now on the last of hers,
 By the moon's cold shine ;
It is the one remaining page
Out of the many shallow and sage
 Whereto she set her sign.
Who could foresee there were to be
 Such missives of pain and pine
Ere I should read this last of hers
 By the moon's cold shine !

'I am playing my oldest tunes,' declared she,
    'All the old tunes I know, —
Those I learnt ever so long ago.'
— Why she should think just then she'd play them
    Silence cloaks like snow.

When I returned from the town at nightfall
    Notes continued to pour
As when I had left two hours before :
'It's the very last time,' she said in closing ;
    'From now I play no more.'

A few morns onward found her fading,
    And, as her life outflew,
I thought of her playing her tunes right through ;
And I felt she had known of what was coming,
    And wondered how she knew.

60. THE PEACE-OFFERING

It was but a little thing,
Yet I knew it meant to me
Ease from what had given a sting
To the very birdsinging
    Latterly.

But I would not welcome it ;
And for all I then declined
O the regrettings infinite
When the night-processions flit
    Through the mind !

61. AN UPBRAIDING

Now I am dead you sing to me
    The songs we used to know,
But while I lived you had no wish
    Or care for doing so.

Now I am dead you come to me
    In the moonlight, comfortless ;
Ah, what would I have given alive
    To win such tenderness !

When you are dead, and stand to me
    Not differenced, as now,
But like again, will you be cold
    As when we lived, or how ?

62. PENANCE

'Why do you sit, O pale thin man,
　　At the end of the room
By that harpsichord, built on the quaint old plan ?
　　— It is cold as a tomb,
And there's not a spark within the grate ;
　　And the jingling wires
　　Are as vain desires
　　That have lagged too late.'

'Why do I ? Alas, far times ago
　　A woman lyred here
In the evenfall ; one who fain did so
　　From year to year ;
And, in loneliness bending wistfully,
　　Would wake each note
　　In sick sad rote,
　　None to listen or see !

'I would not join. I would not stay,
　　But drew away,
Though the winter fire beamed brightly. . . . Aye !
　　I do to-day
What I would not then ; and the chill old keys,
　　Like a skull's brown teeth
　　Loose in their sheath,
　　Freeze my touch ; yes, freeze.'

I look in her face and say,
  'Sing as you used to sing
   About Love's blossoming' ;
But she hints not Yea or Nay.

'Sing, then, that Love's a pain,
  If, Dear, you think it so,
   Whether it be or no ;'
But dumb her lips remain.

I go to a far-off room,
  A faint song ghosts my ear ;
   Which song I cannot hear,
But it seems to come from a tomb.

64. THE PROPHETESS

'Now shall I sing
That pretty thing
"The Mocking-Bird" ?' — And sing it straight did she.
I had no cause
To think it was
A Mocking-bird in truth that sang to me.

Not even the glance
She threw askance
Foretold to me, nor did the tune or rhyme,
That the words bore
A meaning more
Than that they were a ditty of the time.

But after years
Of hopes and fears,
And all they bring, and all they take away,
I found I had heard
The Mocking-bird
In person singing there to me that day.

65. THE STRANGE HOUSE

(Max Gate, a.d. 2000)

'I hear the piano playing —
  Just as a ghost might play.'
'— O, but what are you saying ?
  There's no piano to-day ;
Their old one was sold and broken ;
  Years past it went amiss.'
'— I heard it, or shouldn't have spoken :
  A strange house, this !

'I catch some undertone here,
  From someone out of sight.'
'— Impossible ; we are alone here,
  And shall be through the night.'
'— The parlour-door — what stirred it ?'
  '— No one : no soul's in range.'
'— But, anyhow, I heard it,
  And it seems strange !

'Seek my own room I cannot —
  A figure is on the stair !'
'— What figure ? Nay, I scan not
  Any one lingering there.
A bough outside is waving,
  And that's its shade by the moon.'
'— Well, all is strange ! I am craving
  Strength to leave soon.'

'— Ah, maybe you've some vision
   Of showings beyond our sphere ;
Some sight, sense, intuition
   Of what once happened here ?
The house is old ; they've hinted
   It once held two love-thralls,
And they may have imprinted
      Their dreams on its walls ?

'They were — I think 'twas told me —
   Queer in their works and ways ;
The teller would often hold me
   With weird tales of those days.
Some folk can not abide here,
   But we — we do not care
Who loved, laughed, wept, or died here,
      Knew joy, or despair.'

66. THE WALK

You did not walk with me
Of late to the hill-top tree
   By the gated ways,
   As in earlier days ;
   You were weak and lame,
   So you never came,
And I went alone, and I did not mind,
Not thinking of you as left behind.

I walked up there to-day
Just in the former way ;
   Surveyed around
   The familiar ground
   By myself again :
   What difference, then ?
Only that underlying sense
Of the look of a room on returning thence.

Here by the moorway you returned,
And saw the borough lights ahead
That lit your face — all undiscerned
To be in a week the face of the dead,
And you told of the charm of that haloed view
That never again would beam on you.

And on your left you passed the spot
Where eight days later you were to lie,
And be spoken of as one who was not ;
Beholding it with a heedless eye
As alien from you, though under its tree
You soon would halt everlastingly.

I drove not with you. . . . Yet had I sat
At your side that eve I should not have seen
That the countenance I was glancing at
Had a last-time look in the flickering sheen,
Nor have read the writing upon your face,
'I go hence soon to my resting-place ;

'You may miss me then. But I shall not know
How many times you visit me there,
Or what your thoughts are, or if you go
There never at all.   And I shall not care.
Should you censure me I shall take no heed,
And even your praises no more shall need.'

True : never you'll know.   And you will not mind.
But shall I then slight you because of such ?
Dear ghost, in the past did you ever find
The thought 'What profit', move me much ?
Yet abides the fact, indeed the same, —
You are past love, praise, indifference, blame.

68. BEST TIMES

We went a day's excursion to the stream,
Basked by the bank, and bent to the ripple-gleam,
      And I did not know
      That life would show,
However it might flower, no finer glow.

I walked in the Sunday sunshine by the road
That wound towards the wicket of your abode,
      And I did not think
      That life would shrink
To nothing ere it shed a rosier pink.

Unlooked for I arrived on a rainy night,
And you hailed me at the door by the swaying light
      And I full forgot
      That life might not
Again be touching that ecstatic height.

And that calm eve when you walked up the stair,
After a gaiety prolonged and rare,
      No thought soever
      That you might never
Walk down again, struck me as I stood there.

69. THE GOING

Why did you give no hint that night
That quickly after the morrow's dawn,
And calmly, as if indifferent quite,
You would close your term here, up and be gone
      Where I could not follow
      With wing of swallow
To gain one glimpse of you ever anon !

      Never to bid good-bye,
      Or lip me the softest call,
Or utter a wish for a word, while I
Saw morning harden upon the wall,
      Unmoved, unknowing
      That your great going
Had place that moment, and altered all.

Why do you make me leave the house
And think for a breath it is you I see
At the end of the alley of bending boughs
Where so often at dusk you used to be ;
      Till in darkening dankness
      The yawning blankness
Of the perspective sickens me !

      You were she who abode
      By those red-veined rocks far West,
      You were the swan-necked one who rode
Along the beetling Beeny Crest,
      And, reining nigh me,
      Would muse and eye me,
While Life unrolled us its very best.

Why, then, latterly did we not speak,
Did we not think of those days long dead,
And ere your vanishing strive to seek
That time's renewal ?   We might have said,
     'In this bright spring weather
     We'll visit together
Those places that once we visited.'

     Well, well ! All's past amend,
     Unchangeable.   It must go.
I seem but a dead man held on end
To sink down soon. . . . O you could not know
     That such swift fleeing
     No soul foreseeing —
Not even I — would undo me so !

70. WITHOUT CEREMONY

It was your way, my dear,
To vanish without a word
When callers, friends, or kin
Had left, and I hastened in
To rejoin you, as I inferred.

And when you'd a mind to career
Off anywhere — say to town —
You were all on a sudden gone
Before I had thought thereon,
Or noticed your trunks were down.

So, now that you disappear
For ever in that swift style,
Your meaning seems to be
Just as it used to be :
'Good-bye is not worth while !'

Do you recall
That day in Fall
When we walked towards Saint Alban's Head,
On thistledown that summer had shed,
Or must I remind you ?
Winged thistle-seeds which hitherto
Had lain as none were there, or few,
But rose at the brush of your petticoat-seam
(As ghosts might rise of the recent dead),
And sailed on the breeze in a nebulous stream
Like a comet's tail behind you :
You don't recall
That day in Fall ?

Then do you remember
That sad November
When you left me never to see me more,
And looked quite other than theretofore,
As if it could not *be* you ?
And lay by the window whence you had gazed
So many times when blamed or praised,
Morning or noon, through years and years,
Accepting the gifts that Fortune bore,
Sharing, enduring, joys, hopes, fears !
Well : I never more did see you. —
Say you remember
That sad November !

72. A CIRCULAR

As 'legal representative'
I read a missive not my own,
On new designs the senders give
    For clothes, in tints as shown.

Here figure blouses, gowns for tea,
And presentation-trains of state,
Charming ball-dresses, millinery,
    Warranted up to date.

And this gay-pictured, spring-time shout
Of Fashion, hails what lady proud ?
Her who before last year ebbed out
    Was costumed in a shroud.

73. TWO LIPS

I kissed them in fancy as I came
Away in the morning glow :
I kissed them through the glass of her picture-frame :
She did not know.

I kissed them in love, in troth, in laughter,
When she knew all ; long so !
That I should kiss them in a shroud thereafter
She did not know.

The kiss had been given and taken,
    And gathered to many past :
It never could reawaken ;
    But I heard none say : 'It's the last !'

The clock showed the hour and the minute
    But I did not turn and look :
I read no finis in it,
    As at closing of a book.

But I read it all too rightly
    When, at a time anon,
A figure lay stretched out whitely,
    And I stood looking thereon.

75. A LEAVING

Knowing what it bore
I watched the rain-smitten back of the car —
(Brown-curtained, such as the old ones were) —
When it started forth for a journey afar
Into the sullen November air,
And passed the glistening laurels and round the bend.

I have seen many gayer vehicles turn that bend
In autumn, winter, and summer air,
Bearing for journeys near or afar
Many who now are not, but were,
But I don't forget that rain-smitten car,
Knowing what it bore !

Clouds spout upon her
   Their waters amain
   In ruthless disdain, —
Her who but lately
   Had shivered with pain
As at touch of dishonour
If there had lit on her
So coldly, so straightly
   Such arrows of rain :

One who to shelter
   Her delicate head
Would quicken and quicken
   Each tentative tread
If drops chanced to pelt her
   That summertime spills
   In dust-paven rills
When thunder-clouds thicken
   And birds close their bills.

Would that I lay there
   And she were housed here !
Or better, together
Were folded away there
Exposed to one weather
We both, — who would stray there
When sunny the day there,
   Or evening was clear
   At the prime of the year.

Soon will be growing
   Green blades from her mound,
And daisies be showing
   Like stars on the ground,
Till she form part of them —
Ay — the sweet heart of them,
Loved beyond measure
With a child's pleasure
   All her life's round.

77. 'MY SPIRIT WILL NOT HAUNT THE MOUND'

My spirit will not haunt the mound
    Above my breast,
But travel, memory-possessed,
To where my tremulous being found
    Life largest, best.

My phantom-footed shape will go
    When nightfall grays
Hither and thither along the ways
I and another used to know
    In backward days.

And there you'll find me, if a jot
    You still should care
For me, and for my curious air ;
If otherwise, then I shall not,
    For you, be there.

I found her out there
On a slope few see,
That falls westwardly
To the salt-edged air
Where the ocean breaks
On the purple strand,
And the hurricane shakes
The solid land.

I brought her here,
And have laid her to rest
In a noiseless nest
No sea beats near.
She will never be stirred
In her loamy cell
By the waves long heard
And loved so well.

So she does not sleep
By those haunted heights
The Atlantic smites
And the blind gales sweep,
Whence she often would gaze
At Dundagel's famed head,
While the dipping blaze
Dyed her face fire-red ;

And would sigh at the tale
Of sunk Lyonnesse,
As a wind-tugged tress
Flapped her cheek like a flail ;
Or listen at whiles
With a thought-bound brow
To the murmuring miles
She is far from now.

Yet her shade, maybe,
Will creep underground
Till it catch the sound
Of that western sea
As it swells and sobs
Where she once domiciled,
And joy in its throbs
With the heart of a child.

79. THE RIDDLE

Stretching eyes west
Over the sea,
Wind foul or fair,
Always stood she
Prospect-impressed ;
Solely out there
Did her gaze rest,
Never elsewhere
Seemed charm to be.

Always eyes east
Ponders she now —
As in devotion —
Hills of blank brow
Where no waves plough.
Never the least
Room for emotion
Drawn from the ocean
Does she allow.

80. LOUIE

I am forgetting Louie the buoyant ;
Why not raise her phantom, too,
    Here in daylight
    With the elect one's ?
She will never thrust the foremost figure out of view !

Mid this heat, in gauzy muslin,
See I Louie's life-lit brow
    Here in daylight
    By the elect one's. —
Long two strangers they and far apart ; such neighbours
                now !

I am laughing by the brook with her,
  Splashed in its tumbling stir ;
And then it is a blankness looms
  As if I walked not there,
Nor she, but found me in haggard rooms,
  And treading a lonely stair.

With radiant cheeks and rapid eyes
  We sit where none espies ;
Till a harsh change comes edging in
  As no such scene were there,
But winter, and I were bent and thin,
  And cinder-gray my hair.

We dance in heys around the hall,
  Weightless as thistleball ;
And then a curtain drops between,
  As if I danced not there,
But wandered through a mounded green
  To find her, I knew where.

82. LAMENT

How she would have loved
A party to-day ! —
Bright-hatted and gloved,
With table and tray
And chairs on the lawn
Her smiles would have shone
With welcomings. . . . But
She is shut, she is shut
    From friendship's spell
    In the jailing shell
    Of her tiny cell.

Or she would have reigned
At a dinner to-night
With ardours unfeigned,
And a generous delight ;
All in her abode
She'd have freely bestowed
On her guests. . . . But alas,
She is shut under grass
    Where no cups flow,
    Powerless to know
    That it might be so.

And she would have sought
With a child's eager glance
The shy snowdrops brought
By the new year's advance,
And peered in the rime
Of Candlemas-time
For crocuses . . . chanced
It that she were not tranced
    From sights she loved best ;

Wholly possessed
By an infinite rest !

And we are here staying
Amid these stale things,
Who care not for gaying,
And those junketings
That used so to joy her,
And never to cloy her
As us they cloy ! . . . But
She is shut, she is shut
    From the cheer of them, dead
    To all done and said
    In her yew-arched bed.

The curtains now are drawn,
And the spindrift strikes the glass,
Blown up the jaggèd pass
By the surly salt sou'-west,
And the sneering glare is gone
Behind the yonder crest,
    While she sings to me :
'O the dream that thou art my Love, be it thine,
And the dream that I am thy Love, be it mine,
And death may come, but loving is divine.'

I stand here in the rain,
With its smite upon her stone,
And the grasses that have grown
Over women, children, men,
And their texts that 'Life is vain' ;
But I hear the notes as when
    Once she sang to me :
'O the dream that thou art my Love, be it thine,
And the dream that I am thy Love, be it mine,
And death may come, but loving is divine.'

84. 'SOMETHING TAPPED'

Something tapped on the pane of my room
   When there was never a trace
Of wind or rain, and I saw in the gloom
   My weary Belovéd's face.

'O I am tired of waiting,' she said,
   'Night, morn, noon, afternoon ;
So cold it is in my lonely bed,
     And I thought you would join me soon !'

I rose and neared the window-glass,
   But vanished thence had she :
Only a pallid moth, alas,
   Tapped at the pane for me.

Woman much missed, how you call to me, call to me,
Saying that now you are not as you were
When you had changed from the one who was all to me,
But as at first, when our day was fair.

Can it be you that I hear ? Let me view you, then,
Standing as when I drew near to the town
Where you would wait for me : yes, as I knew you then,
Even to the original air-blue gown !

Or is it only the breeze, in its listlessness
Travelling across the wet mead to me here,
You being ever dissolved to wan wistlessness,
Heard no more again far or near ?

    Thus I ; faltering forward,
    Leaves around me falling,
Wind oozing thin through the thorn from norward,
    And the woman calling.

86. WHEN DEAD

To ——

It will be much better when
        I am under the bough ;
I shall be more myself, Dear, then,
        Than I am now.

No sign of querulousness
        To wear you out
Shall I show there : strivings and stress
        Be quite without.

This fleeting life-brief blight
        Will have gone past
When I resume my old and right
        Place in the Vast.

And when you come to me
        To show you true,
Doubt not I shall infallibly
        Be waiting you.

The twigs of the birch imprint the December sky
   Like branching veins upon a thin old hand ;
I think of summer-time, yes, of last July,
    When she was beneath them, greeting a gathered band
       Of the urban and bland.

Iced airs wheeze through the skeletoned hedge from the north,
   With steady snores, and a numbing that threatens snow,
And skaters pass ; and merry boys go forth
    To look for slides.   But well, well do I know
       Whither I would go !

88. END OF THE YEAR 1912

You were here at his young beginning,
   You are not here at his agèd end ;
Off he coaxed you from Life's mad spinning,
   Lest you should see his form extend
      Shivering, sighing,
      Slowly dying,
   And a tear on him expend.

So it comes that we stand lonely
   In the star-lit avenue,
Dropping broken lipwords only,
   For we hear no songs from you,
      Such as flew here
      For the new year
   Once, while six bells swung thereto.

'What's the good of going to Ridgeway,
    Cerne, or Sydling Mill,
    Or to Yell'ham Hill,
Blithely bearing Casterbridge-way
    As we used to do ?
She will no more climb up there,
Or be visible anywhere
    In those haunts we knew.'

But to-night, while walking weary,
    Near me seemed her shade,
    Come as 'twere to upbraid
This my mood in deeming dreary
    Scenes that used to please ;
And, if she did come to me,
Still solicitous, there may be
    Good in going to these.

So, I'll care to roam to Ridgeway,
    Cerne, or Sydling Mill,
    Or to Yell'ham Hill,
Blithely bearing Casterbridge-way
    As we used to do,
Since her phasm may flit out there,
And may greet me anywhere
    In those haunts we knew.

But don't you know it, my dear,
    Don't you know it,
That this day of the year
(What rainbow-rays embow it !)
We met, strangers confessed,
    But parted — blest ?

Though at this query, my dear,
    There in your frame
Unmoved you still appear,
You must be thinking the same,
But keep that look demure
    Just to allure.

And now at length a trace
    I surely vision
Upon that wistful face
Of old-time recognition,
Smiling forth, 'Yes, as you say,
    It is the day.'

For this one phase of you
    Now left on earth
This great date must endue
With pulsings of rebirth ? —
I see them vitalize
    Those two deep eyes !

But if this face I con
    Does not declare
Consciousness living on
Still in it, little I care
To live myself, my dear,
    Lone-labouring here !

When the spring comes round, and a certain day
Looks out from the brume by the eastern copsetrees
  And says, Remember,
 I begin again, as if it were new,
 A day of like date I once lived through,
 Whiling it hour by hour away ;
  So shall I do till my December,
   When spring comes round.

I take my holiday then and my rest
Away from the dun life here about me,
  Old hours re-greeting
 With the quiet sense that bring they must
 Such throbs as at first, till I house with dust,
 And in the numbness my heartsome zest
  For things that were, be past repeating
   When spring comes round.

Hereto I come to view a voiceless ghost ;
    Whither, O whither will its whim now draw me ?
Up the cliff, down, till I'm lonely, lost,
    And the unseen waters' ejaculations awe me.
Where you will next be there's no knowing,
    Facing round about me everywhere,
        With your nut-coloured hair,
And gray eyes, and rose-flush coming and going.

Yes : I have re-entered your olden haunts at last ;
    Through the years, through the dead scenes I have tracked
        you ;
What have you now found to say of our past —
    Scanned across the dark space wherein I have lacked you ?
Summer gave us sweets, but autumn wrought division ?
    Things were not lastly as firstly well
        With us twain, you tell ?
But all's closed now, despite Time's derision.

I see what you are doing : you are leading me on
    To the spots we knew when we haunted here together,
The waterfall, above which the mist-bow shone
    At the then fair hour in the then fair weather,
And the cave just under, with a voice still so hollow
    That it seems to call out to me from forty years ago,
        When you were all aglow,
And not the thin ghost that I now fraily follow !

Ignorant of what there is flitting here to see,
    The waked birds preen and the seals flop lazily ;
Soon you will have, Dear, to vanish from me,
    For the stars close their shutters and the dawn whitens
        hazily.
Trust me, I mind not, though Life lours,
    The bringing me here ; nay, bring me here again !
        I am just the same as when
Our days were a joy, and our paths through flowers.

He does not think that I haunt here nightly :
    How shall I let him know
That whither his fancy sets him wandering
    I, too, alertly go ? —
Hover and hover a few feet from him
    Just as I used to do,
But cannot answer the words he lifts me —
    Only listen thereto !

When I could answer he did not say them :
    When I could let him know
How I would like to join in his journeys
    Seldom he wished to go.
Now that he goes and wants me with him
    More than he used to do,
Never he sees my faithful phantom
    Though he speaks thereto.

Yes, I companion him to places
    Only dreamers know,
Where the shy hares print long paces,
    Where the night rooks go ;
Into old aisles where the past is all to him,
    Close as his shade can do,
Always lacking the power to call to him,
    Near as I reach thereto !

What a good haunter I am, O tell him !
    Quickly make him know
If he but sigh since my loss befell him
    Straight to his side I go.
Tell him a faithful one is doing
    All that love can do
Still that his path may be worth pursuing,
    And to bring peace thereto.

94. THE WEST-OF-WESSEX GIRL

A very West-of-Wessex girl,
    As blithe as blithe could be,
    Was once well-known to me,
And she would laud her native town,
    And hope and hope that we
Might sometime study up and down
    Its charms in company.

But never I squired my Wessex girl
    In jaunts to Hoe or street
    When hearts were high in beat,
Nor saw her in the marbled ways
    Where market-people meet
That in her bounding early days
    Were friendly with her feet.

Yet now my West-of-Wessex girl,
    When midnight hammers slow
    From Andrew's, blow by blow,
As phantom draws me by the hand
    To the place — Plymouth Hoe —
Where side by side in life, as planned,
    We never were to go !

I reach the marble-streeted town,
     Whose 'Sound' outbreathes its air
          Of sharp sea-salts ;
I see the movement up and down
          As when she was there.
Ships of all countries come and go,
     The bandsmen boom in the sun
          A throbbing waltz ;
The schoolgirls laugh along the Hoe
          As when she was one.

I move away as the music rolls :
     The place seems not to mind
          That she — of old
The brightest of its native souls —
          Left it behind !
Over this green aforedays she
     On light treads went and came.
          Yea, times untold ;
Yet none here knows her history —
          Has heard her name.

'A spirit passed before my face; the hair of my flesh stood up.'

And the Spirit said,
'I can make the clock of the years go backward,
But am loth to stop it where you will.'
And I cried, 'Agreed
To that.   Proceed :
It's better than dead !'

He answered, 'Peace' ;
And called her up — as last before me ;
Then younger, younger she freshed, to the year
I first had known
Her woman-grown,
And I cried, 'Cease ! —

'Thus far is good —
It is enough — let her stay thus always !'
But alas for me — He shook his head :
No stop was there ;
And she waned child-fair,
And to babyhood.

Still less in mien
To my great sorrow became she slowly,
And smalled till she was nought at all
In this checkless griff ;
And it was as if
She had never been.

'Better,' I plained,
'She were dead as before !   The memory of her
Had lived in me ; but it cannot now !'
And coldly his voice :
'It was your choice
To mar the ordained.'

I come across from Mellstock while the moon wastes weaker
To behold where I lived with you for twenty years and more :
I shall go in the gray, at the passing of the mail-train,
And need no setting open of the long familiar door
   As before.

The change I notice in my once own quarters !
A formal-fashioned border where the daisies used to be,
The rooms new painted, and the pictures altered,
And other cups and saucers, and no cosy nook for tea
   As with me.

I discern the dim faces of the sleep-wrapt servants ;
They are not those who tended me through feeble hours and
  strong ;
But strangers quite, who never knew my rule here,
Who never saw me painting, never heard my softling song
   Float along.

So I don't want to linger in this re-decked dwelling,
I feel too uneasy at the contrasts I behold,
And I make again for Mellstock to return here never,
And rejoin the roomy silence, and the mute and manifold
   Souls of old.

'I mean to build a hall anon,
  And shape two turrets there,
  And a broad newelled stair,
And a cool well for crystal water ;
  Yes ; I will build a hall anon,
  Plant roses love shall feed upon,
  And apple-trees and pear.'

He set to build the manor-hall,
  And shaped the turrets there,
  And the broad newelled stair,
And the cool well for crystal water ;
  He built for me that manor-hall,
  And planted many trees withal,
  But no rose anywhere.

And as he planted never a rose
  That bears the flower of love,
  Though other flowers throve
Some heart-bane moved our souls to sever
  Since he had planted never a rose ;
  And misconceits raised horrid shows,
  And agonies came thereof.

'I'll mend these miseries,' then said I,
  And so, at dead of night,
  I went and, screened from sight,
That nought should keep our souls in severance,
  I set a rose-bush. 'This,' said I,
  'May end divisions dire and wry,
  And long-drawn days of blight.'

But I was called from earth — yea, called
    Before my rose-bush grew ;
    And would that now I knew
What feels he of the tree I planted,
    And whether, after I was called
    To be a ghost, he, as of old,
      Gave me his heart anew !

Perhaps now blooms that queen of trees
    I set but saw not grow,
    And he, beside its glow —
Eyes couched of the mis-vision that blurred me —
    Ay, there beside that queen of trees
    He sees me as I was, though sees
      Too late to tell me so !

99. PATHS OF FORMER TIME

No ; no ;
It must not be so :
They are the ways we do not go.

Still chew
The kine, and moo
In the meadows we used to wander through ;

Still purl
The rivulets and curl
Towards the weirs with a musical swirl ;

Haymakers
As in former years
Rake rolls into heaps that the pitchfork rears ;

Wheels crack
On the turfy track
The waggon pursues with its toppling pack.

'Why then shun —
Since summer's not done —
All this because of the lack of one ?'

Had you been
Sharer of that scene
You would not ask while it bites in keen

Why it is so
We can no more go
By the summer paths we used to know !

Unhappy summer you,
　　Who do not see
What your yester-summer saw !
Never, never will you be
　　Its match to me,
　Never, never draw
　Smiles your forerunner drew,
　　Know what it knew !

Divine things done and said
　　Illumined it,
Whose rays crept into corn-brown curls,
Whose breezes heard a humorous wit
　　Of fancy flit. —
　Still the alert brook purls,
　Though feet that there would tread
　　Elsewhere have sped.

So, bran-new summer, you
　　Will never see
All that yester-summer saw !
Never, never will you be
　　In memory
　Its rival, never draw
　Smiles your forerunner drew,
　　Know what it knew !

There you are in the dark,
    Deep in a box
Nobody ever unlocks,
Or even turns to mark ;
    — Out of mind stark.

Yet there you have not been worsed
    Like your sitter
By Time, the Fair's hard-hitter ;
Your beauties, undispersed,
    Glow as at first.

Shut in your case for years,
    Never an eye
Of the many passing nigh,
Fixed on their own affairs,
    Thinks what it nears !

— While you have lain in gloom,
    A form forgot,
Your reign remembered not,
Much life has come to bloom
    Within this room.

Yea, in Time's cyclic sweep
    Unrest has ranged :
Women and men have changed :
Some you knew slumber deep ;
    Some wait for sleep.

When your soft welcomings were said,
This curl was waving on your head,
And when we walked where breakers dinned
It sported in the sun and wind,
And when I had won your words of grace
It brushed and clung about my face.
Then, to abate the misery
Of absentness, you gave it me.

Where are its fellows now ?   Ah, they
For brightest brown have donned a gray,
And gone into a caverned ark,
Ever unopened, always dark !
Yet this one curl, untouched of time,
Beams with live brown as in its prime,
So that it seems I even could now
Restore it to the living brow
By bearing down the western road
Till I had reached your old abode.

Beeny did not quiver,
  Juliot grew not gray,
Thin Vallency's river
  Held its wonted way.
Bos seemed not to utter
  Dimmest note of dirge,
Targan mouth a mutter
  To its creamy surge.

Yet though these, unheeding,
  Listless, passed the hour
Of her spirit's speeding,
  She had, in her flower,
Sought and loved the places —
  Much and often pined
For their lonely faces
  When in towns confined.

Why did not Vallency
  In his purl deplore
One whose haunts were whence he
  Drew his limpid store ?
Why did Bos not thunder,
  Targan apprehend
Body and Breath were sunder
  Of their former friend ?

104. A NIGHT IN NOVEMBER

I marked when the weather changed,
    And the panes began to quake,
And the winds rose up and ranged,
    That night, lying half-awake.

Dead leaves blew into my room,
    And alighted upon my bed,
And a tree declared to the gloom
    Its sorrow that they were shed.

One leaf of them touched my hand,
    And I thought that it was you
There stood as you used to stand,
    And saying at last you knew !

A woman was playing,
    A man looking on ;
    And the mould of her face,
    And her neck, and her hair,
    Which the rays fell upon
    Of the two candles there,
Sent him mentally straying
    In some fancy-place
    Where pain had no trace.

A cowled Apparition
    Came pushing between ;
    And her notes seemed to sigh ;
    And the lights to burn pale,
    As a spell numbed the scene.
    But the maid saw no bale,
And the man no monition ;
    And Time laughed awry,
    And the Phantom hid nigh.

The rain imprinted the step's wet shine
With target-circles that quivered and crossed
As I was leaving this porch of mine ;
When from within there swelled and paused
      A song's sweet note ;
   And back I turned, and thought,
      'Here I'll abide.'

The step shines wet beneath the rain,
Which prints its circles as heretofore ;
I watch them from the porch again,
But no song-notes within the door
      Now call to me
   To shun the dripping lea ;
      And forth I stride.

107. A WOMAN DRIVING

How she held up the horses' heads,
　　Firm-lipped, with steady rein,
Down that grim steep the coastguard treads,
　　Till all was safe again !

With form erect and keen contour
　　She passed against the sea,
And, dipping into the chine's obscure,
　　Was seen no more by me.

To others she appeared anew
　　At times of dusky light,
But always, so they told, withdrew
　　From close and curious sight.

Some said her silent wheels would roll
　　Rutless on softest loam,
And even that her steeds' footfall
　　Sank not upon the foam.

Where drives she now ? It may be where
　　No mortal horses are,
But in a chariot of the air
　　Towards some radiant star.

    I went by the Druid stone
That broods in the garden white and lone,
And I stopped and looked at the shifting shadows
    That at some moments fall thereon
    From the tree hard by with a rhythmic swing,
    And they shaped in my imagining
To the shade that a well-known head and shoulders
    Threw there when she was gardening.

    I thought her behind my back,
    Yea, her I long had learned to lack,
And I said : 'I am sure you are standing behind me,
    Though how do you get into this old track ?'
    And there was no sound but the fall of a leaf
    As a sad response ; and to keep down grief
I would not turn my head to discover
    That there was nothing in my belief.

    Yet I wanted to look and see
    That nobody stood at the back of me ;
But I thought once more : 'Nay, I'll not unvision
    A shape which, somehow, there may be.'
    So I went on softly from the glade,
    And left her behind me throwing her shade,
As she were indeed an apparition —
    My head unturned lest my dream should fade.

There it stands, though alas, what a little of her
    Shows in its cold white look !
Not her glance, glide, or smile ; not a tittle of her
    Voice like the purl of a brook ;
    Not her thoughts, that you read like a book.

It may stand for her once in November
    When first she breathed, witless of all ;
Or in heavy years she would remember
    When circumstance held her in thrall ;
    Or at last, when she answered her call !

Nothing more.   The still marble, date-graven,
    Gives all that it can, tersely lined ;
That one has at length found the haven
    Which every one other will find ;
    With silence on what shone behind.

ST. JULIOT : *September 8,* 1916

I chiselled her monument
  To my mind's content,
Took it to the church by night,
When her planet was at its height,
And set it where I had figured the place in the daytime.
    Having niched it there
I stepped back, cheered, and thought its outlines fair,
    And its marbles rare.

Then laughed she over my shoulder as in our Maytime:
  'It spells not me!' she said:
'Tells nothing about my beauty, wit, or gay time
  With all those, quick and dead,
  Of high or lowlihead,
    That hovered near,
Including you, who carve there your devotion;
  But you felt none, my dear!'

And then she vanished. Checkless sprang my emotion
    And forced a tear
At seeing I'd not been truly known by her,
And never prized! — that my memorial here,
  To consecrate her sepulchre,
    Was scorned, almost,
    By her sweet ghost:
Yet I hoped not quite, in her very innermost!

Can it be so ? It must be so,
That visions have not ceased to be
In this the chiefest sanctuary
Of her whose form we used to know.
— Nay, but her dust is far away,
And 'where her dust is, shapes her shade,
If spirit clings to flesh,' they say :
Yet here her life-parts most were played !

Her voice explored this atmosphere,
Her foot impressed this turf around,
Her shadow swept this slope and mound,
Her fingers fondled blossoms here ;
And so, I ask, why, why should she
Haunt elsewhere, by a slighted tomb,
When here she flourished sorrow-free,
And, save for others, knew no gloom ?

This after-sunset is a sight for seeing,
Cliff-heads of craggy cloud surrounding it.
  — And dwell you in that glory-show ?
You may ; for there are strange strange things in being,
    Stranger than I know.

Yet if that chasm of splendour claim your presence
Which glows between the ash cloud and the dun,
  How changed must be your mortal mould !
Changed to a firmament-riding earthless essence
    From what you were of old :

All too unlike the fond and fragile creature
Then known to me. . . . Well, shall I say it plain ?
  I would not have you thus and there,
But still would grieve on, missing you, still feature
    You as the one you were.

If you had known
When listening with her to the far-down moan
Of the white-selvaged and empurpled sea,
And rain came on that did not hinder talk,
Or damp your flashing facile gaiety
In turning home, despite the slow wet walk
By crooked ways, and over stiles of stone ;
       If you had known

      You would lay roses,
Fifty years thence, on her monument, that discloses
Its graying shape upon the luxuriant green ;
Fifty years thence to an hour, by chance led there,
What might have moved you ? — yea, had you foreseen
That on the tomb of the selfsame one, gone where
The dawn of every day is as the close is,
      You would lay roses !

The dark was thick.   A boy he seemed at that time
  Who trotted by me with uncertain air ;
'I'll tell my tale,' he murmured, 'for I fancy
    A friend goes there ? . . .'

Then thus he told.   'I reached — 'twas for the first time —
  A dwelling.   Life was clogged in me with care ;
I thought not I should meet an eyesome maiden,
    But found one there.

'I entered on the precincts for the second time —
  'Twas an adventure fit and fresh and fair —
I slackened in my footsteps at the porchway,
    And found her there.

'I rose and travelled thither for the third time,
  The hope-hues growing gayer and yet gayer
As I hastened round the boscage of the outskirts,
    And found her there.

'I journeyed to the place again the fourth time
  (The best and rarest visit of the rare,
As it seemed to me, engrossed about these goings),
    And found her there.

'When I bent me to my pilgrimage the fifth time
  (Soft-thinking as I journeyed I would dare
A certain word at token of good auspice),
    I found her there.

'That landscape did I traverse for the sixth time,
  And dreamed on what we purposed to prepare ;
I reached a tryst before my journey's end came,
    And found her there.

'I went again — long after — aye, the seventh time ;
    The look of things was sinister and bare
As I caught no customed signal, heard no voice call,
        Nor found her there.

'And now I gad the globe — day, night, and any time,
    To light upon her hiding unaware,
And, maybe, I shall nigh me to some nymph-niche,
        And find her there !'

'But how,' said I, 'has your so little lifetime
    Given roomage for such loving, loss, despair ?
A boy so young !'   Forthwith I turned my lantern
        Upon him there.

His head was white.   His small form, fine aforetime,
    Was shrunken with old age and battering wear,
An eighty-years long plodder saw I pacing
        Beside me there.

115. TEN YEARS SINCE

'Tis ten years since
I saw her on the stairs,
Heard her in house-affairs,
And listened to her cares ;
And the trees are ten feet taller,
And the sunny spaces smaller
Whose bloomage would enthrall her ;
And the piano wires are rustier,
The smell of bindings mustier,
And lofts and lumber dustier
Than when, with casual look
And ear, light note I took
Of what shut like a book
Those ten years since !

November 1922

She opened the door of the West to me,
  With its loud sea-lashings,
  And cliff-side clashings
Of waters rife with revelry.

She opened the door of Romance to me,
  The door from a cell
  I had known too well,
Too long, till then, and was fain to flee.

She opened the door of a Love to me,
  That passed the wry
  World-welters by
As far as the arching blue the lea.

She opens the door of the Past to me,
  Its magic lights,
  Its heavenly heights,
When forward little is to see !

BIBLIOGRAPHY

J. E. Barton, 'A Chapter on the Poetry', in *The Art of Thomas Hardy*, by Lionel Johnson : New York, Dodd, Mead, 1923.

Edmund Blunden, *Thomas Hardy* (EML series) : London, Macmillan, 1941.

Samuel C. Chew, *Thomas Hardy, Poet and Novelist* : New York, Knopf, 1929.

Vere H. Collins, *Talks with Thomas Hardy* : London, Duckworth, 1928.

Edmund Gosse, 'The Lyrical Poetry of Thomas Hardy', in *Some Diversions of a Man of Letters* : London, Heinemann, 1919.

Peter Green, *Kenneth Grahame* : London, John Murray, 1959.

Emma Hardy, *Some Recollections* : London, Oxford University Press, 1961.

Florence Emily Hardy, *The Early Life of Thomas Hardy* : London, Macmillan, 1928.

Florence Emily Hardy, *The Later Years of Thomas Hardy* : London, Macmillan, 1930.

Florence Emily Hardy : *The Life of Thomas Hardy* : London, Macmillan, 1962.

Thomas Hardy : *Collected Poems* : London, Macmillan, fourth edition, 1930.

Thomas Hardy : '*Dearest Emmie*' : *Letters to his First Wife* : London, Macmillan, 1963.

Thomas Hardy, *Letters*, edited by Carl J. Weber, Waterville, Maine : Colby College Press, 1954.

Arthur McDowall, *Thomas Hardy, a Critical Study* : London, Faber, 1931.

Arthur McDowall, 'Thomas Hardy's Poetry', *Times Literary Supplement*, London, 26 January 1928.

Henry W. Nevinson, *Thomas Hardy* : London, George Allen & Unwin, [1941].

William Lyon Phelps, *Autobiography with Letters* : New York, Oxford University Press, 1939.

Richard Little Purdy, *Thomas Hardy : A Bibliographical Study* : London, Oxford University Press, 1954.

Siegfried Sassoon, *Siegfried's Journey* : New York, The Viking Press, 1946.

Carl J. Weber, *Hardy and the Lady from Madison Square* : Waterville, Maine, Colby College Press, 1952.

Carl J. Weber, *Hardy of Wessex* : New York, Columbia University Press, 1940 ; Hamden, Connecticut, Archon Books, 1962.

Carl J. Weber, *The Rise and Fall of James Ripley Osgood* (Hardy's Publisher) : Waterville, Colby College Press, 1959.

Frederick Wedmore, 'Thomas Hardy's Poems', in *Certain Comments* : London, Selwyn & Blount, 1925.

Edith Wharton, *Eternal Passion in English Poetry* (pages 76-77) : New York, D. Appleton—Century Company, 1939.

G. M. Young, 'Introduction [to Hardy's Poetry]', *Selected Poems of Thomas Hardy* : London, Macmillan, 1940.

INDEX OF TITLES

243

INDEX OF FIRST LINES

GENERAL INDEX